What readers a
God's Path to Golden Splendor

"***God's Path to Golden Splendor*** is God's gift to every generation. It is a must read! I picked it up from a friend, and couldn't put it down. I read it through the night finally finishing it at about 4:00 a.m. I enjoy books that teach me something, that make me cry, that make me think, that cause me to see Christ more clearly through the testimonies of His children, and I recommend this book in its entirety. I bought 15 copies of this book for gifts because of its incredible wisdom.—**Teri**

"As I read ***God's Path to Golden Splendor*** I often was reminded of attitudes that I need to remember in my walk with the LORD. It is excellent advice on growing old gracefully, plus…start NOW!

…It would be best if this book could find its way to those of us in our 50s, 60s, and 70s. The earlier the better!"—**Damon**

"***God's Path to Golden Splendor*** is wonderful! I truly appreciated every chapter, and I know the heart that is seeking a life that honors and brings glory to God, right up to the end, will enjoy and benefit from it. I could feel my own heartbeat so often…I kept thinking what a great Group Study this could be to encourage and help one another along. My heart was touched and convicted and motivated! I was encouraged by the entire format, and especially the prayers and the songs that touched my emotions so deeply; and…I just know that every word is right on track!"—**Jane**

"Your hammer really knows where the nail head is!…***God's Path to Golden Splendor*** is beautiful!…It raised a banner of challenge for me."—**Jack**

"…***God's Path to Golden Splendor***…helped me think about what I really want to claim at the end of my life, and made real what my hopes and goals ought to be."—**Julie**

"…thank you! The light you have shined on my life has reminded me to polish off my sword and fight the wolf threatening to consume me. I am MUCH younger than most readers, and just starting my family, but ***God's Path to Golden Splendor*** has ignited a fire in my heart that I pray will burn with such passion and light in the decades to come."—**Grace**

God's Path to Golden Splendor

Perfected by HIS Power

By
Jacki Martin

To Ron "Lou" + Linda,
May God bless
you abundantly as
you continue to
shine forth HIS
glorious, golden
Splendor!
By HIS grace
alone,
Jacki Martin
Ps. 145

MEGASIGHT
Northridge, CA

Third printing, 2017.

Library of Congress TXu1-216-602

ISBN-10: 1547255846
ISBN-13: 9781547255849

Printed in the United States of America

To all my precious friends in the faith
who continue to walk before me
as proof of God's perfecting power.
Their lives show me how to thrive
in the midst of the Refiner's fire,
and come forth as ***Gold****.*

Special Thanks

To my wonderful husband, Dick, and son, Greg,
who have encouraged me, loved me,
and prayed for me every step of the way.
To my Dad and Mom, Jack and Betty Huntsman,
who have always "been there" for me, and support my every effort.

To Jane and Jack York, Damon Loomis and Jim Pile,
who carefully read and reviewed every word,
and are truly four of my most cherished role models.

To Sharon Devol, Bea Becker and Mary Jane Duncan
who skillfully guided me through the process for including
the words of many beloved hymns.

To Joni Eareckson Tada, Bob Vernon,
"C.W." Smith, and countless others,
who have touched my heart with incredible insights
from their own encouraging stories.

To Mr. Glover, Dr. John MacArthur, Bob King, Dr. William Varner, Tom Pennington, Warren Currie, Fletcher Anderson, and many others who have faithfully poured God's Word into my life, year after year.

And in the words of David's Psalm 34:1-3,
"I will bless the **LORD** at all times; His praise shall continually be in my mouth. My soul shall make its boast in the **LORD**; The humble shall hear of it and be glad.
Oh, magnify the **LORD** with me, and let us exalt His Name together."

God's Path to Golden Splendor
Perfected by HIS Power

Contents

God's Path to Golden Splendor

Perfected by HIS Power

By

Jacki Martin

Introduction

gold, n.- 1. a precious yellow metallic element
2. money; wealth; riches.
3. something likened to gold in brightness, preciousness, superiority: a heart of gold.
4. Gold Medal.

"Go for the gold!"

The crowd cheered wildly as the runner's exhausted body broke through the victory ribbon. First place, and the coveted gold medal was no longer just an elusive dream of a youthful mind. All those early hours of hard work had finally paid off. The gold was in hand.

"Go for the gold!"

The excited men surrounded the small printed placard announcing the discovery of gold on the West Coast of North America. Thousands of would-be millionaires raced to California to the tune of "Gold Dust, or Bust!" Hard work and sacrifice paled in the glow of things to come.

"Go for the gold!"

The gold watch glittered in the setting sun. Twenty years of youthful preparation, and forty-five years as a dedicated, hardworking, loyal employee have culminated in this special moment. Freedom from the alarm clock, and the symbol of the golden time to come was finally attained.

Since the discovery of gold on planet Earth it has become the standard by which we gauge and appraise our daily lives. We use "gold" to measure our victories, our money, our emotions and our success. We even call the end of our earthly lives our "Golden Years." Some seekers spend their entire lives chasing after fool's gold, which eventually leads to bitter resentment for a wasted life. For the rest of us, though, pure gold is our goal, and because we have experienced the challenges of life we know that we need a well thought out plan if we truly intend to reach our goal.

Planning for retirement is, or has been, a giant focus in many of our lives. Will we have enough money to last to the end? What about health care, and long-term insurance? Should we do this, or should we do that. What is the best way to insure that our final years will be golden?

Adding to our confusion is an ever-present barrage of new products being peddled at every turn. Most of us have watched hours of commercial television and have been slowly conditioned by the clever and powerful advertising that seems to be focused on our exact "need" of the moment. "You *need* to invest… You *need* to take fiber… You *need* this or that medication for your heartburn, arthritis, joint pain, memory loss, impotence, etc." Every "negative" aspect of the aging process is constantly bombarding our emotions. Whether we realize it or not, the "fear factor" is slowly and continually, drop by drop, filling our "bucket." We start buying into the "wisdom" of the world.

We are slowly becoming victims!

And "they" claim to have all the answers (which we soon realize are temporary, at best).

It seems that Madison Avenue has read John 16:33(NIV), where Jesus warns, "In the world you will have trouble." We can picture all the movers and shakers of the advertising world, sitting around their highly polished conference tables, "brainstorming" the next set of problems and troubles to face the Baby Boomers and their parents. They know from many years of market testing that there is a lot of money to be made when "fear" is the focus. Their skillful abilities capture our attention and draw us to put our trust in the latest human solution for any and every problem. (Some truly helpful; some not!)

In the process, we become more and more convinced of the pending doom of old age. We tend to forget the rest of what Jesus said in John 16:33(NIV). He encourages us with, "But take heart! I have overcome the world."

Imagine if God produced the commercials for aging!

"Old 'Wine,' Aged to Perfection in the Master's Hand!"

"Thankful, Silver Saints Cause Heaven to Sing!"

"Look to Me for a Full and Contented Spirit!"

"My Time Is Your Time! My Friendship Is Intimate and Continually Available!"

"Seek Me! I Will Hold You and Never Forsake You!"

Shortly before Christ was led to the "trouble" of His death on the cross for our salvation, He prayed for His disciples and the troubles they were about to face in His Name. He also prayed for every believer (that's us, if we know Him!) to be protected, not from trouble (He just said we would have it!), but from the "evil one." The "wolf" who is constantly on alert, waiting, watching and working to snatch us away from our eternal Shepherd. With the promise of fool's gold he tries to divert us from our quest for the True Gold. That is, if we allow the world's view of old age to infect us, instead of continually renewing our minds with God's Word.

In the process of trying to avoid the pitfalls of aging, we are subtly becoming "victims" of the aging "monster" that looms before us.

I'm beginning to hear people complaining, and blaming their life-long inadequacies on being old. Things they have had trouble with for years (spilling food, forgetting names and dates, etc.) are now being relegated to the aging process. Finally they can place thc blame outside their own control!

I am not being naïve! I have watched the loss of control, and the indignities suffered in the lives of many of my close relatives. I'm aware of the entropy that is taking place in my own body and mind. I've read Solomon's vivid description of the waning human condition many times. It is not a pretty picture! And yet, for some reason, God has allowed this time in our lives. He is the author of life, whether young or old. He has a purpose for every "test" that is set bcfore us. Let's not fail the test before we even begin, by buying-in to the "victim" mentality of, not just the world's thinking, but also thc "thinking" of well-meaning Christian authors, radio commentators and friends.

Join me in reading Romans 12:1-2 and, daily "submit your bodies (no matter how feeble) as living sacrifices, holy and pleasing to God-for this is your spiritual act of worship. Do not conform any longer to the pattern of the world, but be transformed by the **renewing of your mind**, then you will be able to test and approve what God's will is; His good, pleasing and perfect will."

Remember John the Baptist's admonition (John 3:30), "I must become less [We don't seem to have a choice about this now!], and He must become more [This is where we choose!]."

If we choose to submit, and allow Him to shine through our weakness, we will become the storehouse of His abundant "Gold," and the "Golden Years" will take on a powerful new meaning.

From the very beginning of human history God has put choice into our control. Even though the outlook of aging seems bleak, and our control over our temporal being may one day be usurped by others (our children, caregivers, etc.), if our mental capacities allow us, we will come to our last day with our God-given power of choice intact. We will either choose self-pity and needy indulgence, or we will choose to magnify His most precious Name. When we choose the latter, His Hand will sustain us in mercy and grace, and His smile will encourage and uphold us.

He beckons us to *"Go for the GOLD!"*

The Purpose of this Book

This book was written to act as a guide to God's "gold mine." If, as a miner of God's gold, we allow ourselves to enter the "mine" of the aging process without being properly equipped, we may find ourselves in isolated darkness struggling to simply make it to the end. Our thoughts of magnifying the golden fruit of God's *love, joy, peace, kindness, goodness, gentleness, patience, faithfulness, and self-control* will diminish as we allow ourselves to become "victims" of the darkness.

To get the most out of this situation we must first equip ourselves, and continue to learn to compensate for the problems we will face, and also intentionally plan how to thrive and flourish as we move forward. We don't need to "re-invent the wheel." All of human history has gone into this "mine" before us! Many became self-centered "victims," while others, who consciously took the time to prepare, made the last half of their lives the best half of their lives for the glory of God.

True learning is a choice and an act of the will. It equals information (positive or negative) entering the brain and being stored as memory that is easily accessed for application. "Talking the talk" is always easier than "walking the walk," when it comes to positive applications. As we age, physical walking may become a thing of the past. How will we compensate and give feet to our faith?

It is never too early, or too late to begin, for even in the capable hands of dedicated caretakers, in our last days, this book will bring hope for the future, whether our future equals one day, or many, many years.

How to Use the "Claim Your Gold" Application Guide:

The *"Claim Your Gold"* section of each chapter is an Application Guide that is based on learning techniques that help to embed information for permanent retention more easily. Some of these techniques are: **highlighting,** and **defining** key words, reviewing verses and concepts, re-reading Scripture, **active involvement** in key concepts, **singing**, etc.

When information concerning God's character, laws, and promises becomes entrenched in your soul, the Holy Spirit can bring it to your mind at the needed time. The more you put into your memory, consciously (through reading, listening, and memorizing), or subtly (through note-taking, journaling, discussions and song), the more the Holy Spirit has to work with to conform you to the perfect image of God. Educational studies have shown that different methods of inputting new information produce radically different percentages of retention. Each application capitalizes on using the easiest and most productive methods.

The three applications in the *"Claim Your Gold"* guide include:

– **Engrave your heart** (Scripture Input)

Several key verses that summarize the theme of the chapter are presented in this section. These verses are to be memorized, or simply reread, many times during the day. Studies indicate that when you read new information only one time, you tend to remember about 10% of the content, but as you reread a passage several times a day the path of memory in your brain will be deepened. As the printed material enters your brain through your eyes, retention will be increased to approximately 50% if you also read aloud. Seeing, speaking and hearing information will greatly enhance your memory. Of course, all of this is based on the assumption that you are truly focused and trying to remember. The goal would be to memorize each Scripture.

– **Refine the gold** (Application Points)

The Application Points will help you "walk the talk" of each chapter. Each point will help you apply the concepts in a personal, down-to-earth way, in reading, writing, speaking or action. Living out God's purpose for you is not a spectator sport. If you are willing to take the first step of action God promises He will not forsake you. As you apply and experience learning through actions your memory will jump to about 80%. If you continue to act on what you know, the path of your memory will become well traveled, and deepened. It will facilitate your behavior to become more automatic and natural (pure gold), and less forced or fake (fool's gold).

– **Nuggets of wisdom, promises and praise** (Sing)

One of the most fun and effective ways of storing memory is to put facts and information to music, or summarize it as poetry. How many of us will go to our graves still remembering the "A-B-C" song we learned in kindergarten? Some of us still sing that song (only mentally, I hope!) as we thumb through the phone book or dictionary. Music is a powerful tool that touches our emotions. Emotional-memory is one of the most powerful categories of memory. Is it any wonder that the Bible instructs us, over and over again, to "sing… "sing to the LORD"… "sing!" (Psalm 40:3; 57:9-10; 59:16-17). While singing (or simply reading) praise to the LORD through the carefully chosen hymn at the end of the application section you will acknowledge and remember each chapter's content.

Note to caretakers: Caretakers will obviously have to assess appropriate application of the contents, realizing that some areas will be more beneficial than others at different levels of infirmity. Reading the verses, the prayers, and singing the hymns will always be appropriate.

But… can you really teach an "old dog," new tricks?

The answer is emphatically, ***yes!*** But as that "old dog" ages, its ability to move around and experience new information declines, and as audio and visual impairment limits reading, writing, listening and seeing new stimuli, the "old dog" must refocus. We must be prepared to focus on what works, and not sit and complain about what doesn't work.

To maintain our mental acuity through the coming years, we must tap our God-given gifts and Spirit-given self-control (Gal. 5:22-23) and persevere in faithfulness.

"Remember ***now*** your Creator…" (Eccl. 12:1).

The time is always ***now!***

Now…claim, mine, and refine the gold for *your* "Golden Years." It's never too early to begin to be transformed and perfected—the sooner the better!

Please remember—before you apply any of a chapter's content you must first seek God's guidance and power, through the Scriptures and prayer, to personalize the application. As you learn to examine your daily life, His path for your transformation will be different than His plan for anyone else.

Chapter 1

Not If... But When?

Embrace Your Life Stage

acknowledge, v.- to admit to be true; recognize truth, or fact of.

acceptance, n.- the act of assenting or believing.

I stood there… staring into the mirror… "Who is that looking back at me?"

The eyes and teeth are mine, but what has happened to that smooth, young skin and the firm muscle tone? Many years ago I made a vow to myself that I wouldn't let this happen. I would exercise, eat right, take care of my teeth and skin, take my vitamins and minerals, and drink all the water I could. I would be the Jack La Lanne of my day! I would be in control and wouldn't have to face what I'm looking at now—a sixty-year-old facade with the attitude and thoughts of a much younger person.

It's funny how life has its own ideas. Recently I saw a picture of Jack La Lanne in the newspaper. I had to admit that Jack and I had minimal control over the aging process. Our "control" is limited to either denying it, or acknowledging it, accepting its challenges, and then making the most of it.

I've been teaching now for 40 years in the Los Angeles area. Year after year new, young teachers are hired who become integrated into our school teaching teams. When working together, the age gulf that lies between us always seems to disappear. That is why it shocked me when my team members started opening doors for me as we walked around our campus. The first time it happened I jokingly asked them if they did it out of respect for my position as Lead Teacher. They all looked sheepishly at each other, and then one of them had the courage to tell me that they had been raised to honor and respect their elders.

"What?"

Could this really be happening to someone who has expended incredible energy trying to stay fit? The evidence was there in the mirror before me; I had one foot in the doorway of the "Golden Years" and the other foot on a banana peel. I decided I needed to begin to prepare to end well. How could I end my stint on earth without dishonoring my love for the LORD; without becoming one of those negative, complaining, angry, and ungrateful people we've all had to endure at one time or another? How can I accept this aging process, and follow in the footsteps of my most positive, productive and thankful golden role models?

Solomon said, "Remember, now your creator in the days of your youth before the days of trouble come and the years approach when you will say, 'I find no pleasure in them'…" (Eccl. 12:1(NIV)). I decided when Solomon said "now" he meant NOW! I needed to move into reality and start planning how to find the gold I've heard so much about, and how to pass this final test in obedience to God's plan for me.

I began my preparation by searching the Scriptures for the best way to glorify His precious Name until I take my very last breath.

I found many verses dealing with old age, but I still didn't take them seriously for myself. As I found each "old-age" verse I would jot it down, and then write it in the birthday cards of my wonderful friends who were also involved in this aging process. As they opened their cards we would all laugh and pretend it was only in the Bible for other people.

I began to look for those "other people" and watch to see how they applied those scriptures as their lives ebbed away. What I saw in many people was not pretty. Some of the Christians I had admired (from afar) as my role models in the church were leaving a very "bad taste" in my mouth, and in the mouths of others who were trying to live out their charge of "honor your father and your mother" (Ex. 20:12)...and care for the widows and the fatherless. A number of these older Christians were making the lives of their children and caretakers miserable.

Of course, there were also those precious "silver" saints who allowed the Holy Spirit to control them. They showed evidence of this with every passing day. These were the people I wanted to get close to!

I started seeking the wisdom and insights of older Christian mentors and role models—those who have guided me, by their example, through other "days of trouble." What a joy to be encouraged by people who magnify the LORD, not just with their mouths but also with every fiber of their being.

I pray that God will use this book to help strengthen our example to the next generation(s), as we continue to encourage each other through this final passage of life.

Thank You, LORD, for my life. Show me how to accept each new challenge, and prepare for this final test. Bind me, every day, to Your will and purpose for me. Help me to "still bear fruit in my old age," and "stay fresh and green" (Psalm 92:12-14-NIV). *Teach me to persevere in love, truth, kindness, gentleness, and self-control to the very end of the days You have laid out before me.*

Let my last day be my BEST day!

Let me enter Your gates of glory, and hear those wonderful words from Your own lips... "Well done, My good and faithful servant." (Matthew 25:21)

Claim Your Gold

Application Guide

Not if… But When?

Engrave your heart:
(Memorize, or simply re-read during the day.)

"Remember ***now*** *your Creator in the days of your youth,*
before *the difficult days come, and the years draw near when you say,*
'I have no pleasure them'." -Ecclesiastes 12:1

"Well done, good and faithful servant; you were faithful over a few things,
I will make you ruler over many things.
Enter into the joy of your Lord." -Matthew 25:21

Refine the gold:

1. Carefully consider the words that you would like to hear as you stand before the Lord's Throne for the first time. This is your "epitaph"—your mission statement for your life. It should be very specific: a summary of what you would like to be for the rest of your days.

"Well done, (insert your own name here) ***you****…."*

2. Plan to review your "epitaph" at least once a year, on your birthday, spiritual birthday, anniversary of your baptism, or New

Year's Eve. After a year of growth in the LORD you might find you want to modify it.

Of course we can't put words into our Lord's mouth, but we can seek to please Him (Psalm 19:14).

Nuggets of wisdom, promises and praise:
(Sing, or simply read as prayerful poetry.)

"A Charge to Keep I Have" by Charles Wesley

A charge to keep have I,
A God to glorify,
A never-dying soul to save,
And fit it for the sky.
To serve the present age,
My calling to fulfill;
O may it all my pow'rs engage
To do my Master's will!
Arm me with watchful care
As in Thy sight to live,
And now Thy servant, Lord, prepare
A strict account to give!
Help me to watch and pray,
And still on Thee rely,
O let me not my trust betray,
But press to realms on high.

Chapter 2

The Wolf at the Door

Tackle Self-Centeredness

heart, n.- 1.the center of the total personality, especially with reference to intuition, feeling, or emotion.
2. capacity for sympathy; feeling; affection.
3. spirit, courage, or enthusiasm.

When I was a tiny child I heard the wonderful, and quite scary, tale of *Little Red Riding Hood.* I'm sure you remember it too. Little Red Riding Hood was pictured as a sweet, innocent child braving the unknown dangers of the dark woods to carry a basket full of goodies to her elderly grandmother. As she approached her grandmother's bed she sensed something was wrong. Hoping her grandmother would settle her fears, she asked about all the changes she saw in Granny's appearance. When she started discussing her grandmother's much larger teeth ("Grandma, what large teeth you have!"), the wolf, that had of course just eaten Grandma and was disguised in her bedclothes, seized the moment to devour poor Little Red Riding Hood.

What a premise for a child's story!

I don't know what your parents told you when you woke up screaming because you had just dreamed that the Big Bad Wolf was chasing you around the bedroom trying to gobble you up. My mom and dad comforted me by saying, "It was just a story. There is no such thing as the Big Bad Wolf!"

As I fast forward through my life I've discovered that they were wrong. Through many surveys, research, and personal experience from my life and the lives of my friends, I know that the "Big Bad Wolf" is alive and well! (Matthew 7:15-20)

I've heard many stories through the years of modern day Little Red Riding Hoods who have lovingly gone the extra mile to grandmother's house, toting baskets of kindness and hopefully a little joy. But as it so often happens, even with grandparents and parents who claim to know and love the LORD, the "Big Bad Wolf" has swallowed up the images of the sweet, loving grandparent that we've all seen in those wonderful Norman Rockwell paintings.

As Red approaches the bed with her basket of goodies, she realizes this frail person IS the "Big Bad Wolf." For as she bends to get into Grandma's view, Grandma bites her head off with unkind, unloving and negative words.

"Why don't you ever come to see me?"

"But, Grandma, I'm here now!"

"Don't you know I don't like those cookies?"

"But Grandma, you said you'd rather have these than the ones I brought last time."

"Why are you wearing that hideous red hood? You look like a giant blood clot!"

"But Grandma..."

"Can't you get a better job? What are you thinking, or are you?

"Grandma...!"

"When are you going to get married and settle down?"

"I'm praying and waiting for God's will, Grandma."

"Whatever! Where are my slippers?"

As Little Red bends to find Grandma's slippers she thinks to herself: *O Grandma, what a small heart you have! Where are all those convictions you use to have about reaching out to people and showing them the love of God?*

Is this the way we are all destined to end our days on earth? Will we all destroy our testimonies of God's love in our lives as we endure this last insult to our bodies?

Is old age God's "final exam" for Christians?

All of life is a continual test (Deuteronomy 8:2). Adam and Eve were the first to have their obedience tested (Genesis 3). God's tests not only allow us to prove our obedience to His will for us, but also help to magnify His love, strength, power, peace, joy, and faithfulness in our lives.

How could God prove and demonstrate His character to us if we didn't have a need to be loved, or if our days were constantly filled with sufficient food, satisfaction, and security? Deuteronomy 8:11-20 warns against forgetting God in our daily thoughts. Forgetfulness leads to disobedience. If we never, knowingly, had to depend on God for anything, a sense of self-sufficiency could become our stumbling block. Pride would rule our heart, and most likely we would forget that He is the source of everything.

The following illustration of a diamond salesman has always been one of my favorites.

As the salesman tries to promote the beauty of a diamond ring, he could simply open the little white box and let the customer take a peek, or he could find a much better approach to dramatically display its beauty. For example, he could use a black velvet background with a strong overhead light to illuminate and reflect the magnificence and glory of each facet.

The truth has not changed. The quality of the diamond is the same whether it is displayed in the little white box, or on the blackness of the velvet. But the evidence of its beauty is so much clearer, and seemingly magnified, when it is surrounded by blackness.

The same is true with God's love and power in our lives. He is always with us, but when we start feeling self-sufficient, and we think that our ways are better than His ways, He reminds us of the beauty of His Light by sending the darkness of trials beyond our control. When we turn to Him in these times of weakness and lack of control

His mighty character of love and caring is obvious and magnified in our time of need.

Stories from the Old Testament clearly show us the results of prideful human nature. God blessed His people over and over again with incredible miracles, and yet they continually turned their backs in disobedience. In His great compassion God sent Moses to save the Israelites from lives of darkness, hardship, and slavery (in Exodus). They complained and wanted to be relieved of their position of servitude. God displayed His power and love for the Israelites on the "black background" of ten devastating plagues on the Egyptian nation that He allowed them to view from afar. They "got it" for a short time, but then when their commitment and love for God was tested in the desert they quickly turned to fearful complaining and distrust. At this point God moved the "black backdrop" of trials and tribulations closer to their own experience. Forty years of wandering aimlessly in the desert would purge the unfaithful generation from among God's chosen people.

There are a few people in the world (I Corinthians 10:11; Hebrews 4:11) who actually learn from the tests, mistakes, and problems that others face. These people are in tune, sensitive, and learn quickly through the "lessons" that they "experience" from afar; people for whom the Scriptures come alive. They view the tests of others and make application unto themselves. They see the glory of God in everything—from the ants on the kitchen counter to the awesomeness of the heavens (Psalm 8:1-9) on a cold crisp winter night. They are the "Jobs" and "Ruths" of our time. In everything they give thanks; in everything they find meaning and purpose.

These are people who understand what Solomon discovered in Ecclesiastes. God creates us for His own pleasure. We are to love Him with all our heart and to seek only His desire for our life by keeping His commandments (Eccl. 12:13). After years of searching for meaning and discarding every possibility, Solomon finally came to the end of a life filled with God's blessings and an incredible, unmatched wisdom—he figured it out! God defined the purpose of human life before the beginning of time.

What is more pleasurable and joyful to each of us than to know that another human being loves us with all of his or her whole heart and will bend over backward to show us that love? If we are fortunate, we've all had a small glimpse of this human love in our own lifetime. Someone who has the whole world to choose from to love… but chooses to love us!

To have the love of a faithful dog has always been comforting. All you have to do is throw a little food in a bowl and you have a friend for life. But that isn't the "robot" love for which we were created.

God gave us all the beauty and temptations of His awesome creation, the world. He said, "It's yours! It is very good!"

His greatest joy is when His carefully created children, who have been given all the choices in the universe, choose to love, adore, trust, and obey the One who has brought them to life. That is our purpose! That is what Solomon, with his entire God-given wisdom, finally discovered. We are here to "Fear God and keep His commandments, for this is man's ALL" (Eccl. 12:13). If we don't see this as our God given purpose, we have no purpose! "All is vanity!" (Eccl. 12:8)

Many people come to the door of the "Golden Years" looking for what life can give back to them. They've worked hard all their lives and now it's time to let the world honor them. It's time to find the gold at the end of the rainbow that everyone talks about. They push aside their God-given purpose of praise and obedience, and remind their world that the Bible says to take care of the elderly, the widows, and the fatherless.

It's always easier to sit in church and give someone else the elbow when the preacher is preaching. But as is true in all of life's trials, we are to be thankful (I Thess. 5:18), be still (Psalm 46:10), and be obedient (Deut. 13:4) to the Spirit's leading. Do we want our world to honor us only with their lips, out of duty, or with their hearts, out of truth and love?

While working on this chapter I was "privileged" to witness an exchange between a very duty-bound 60-year-old son and his seemingly needy and frail father. I was sitting with my mother-in-law outside the doctor's office waiting for our ride to return with the car. I watched the son carefully leave his bent and stone-faced father, slumped down in a wheelchair, to run and get their family car. He spoke clearly into his ear to assure him, and calm his complaining, that he would be right back. The father looked dazed and confused. My heart went out to both of them, as the son seemed torn about leaving. I signaled over the father's head that I would watch him.

The minute his "boy" was out of earshot the old man perked up, got out of his wheelchair, walked to the trash can to dispose of a gum wrapper, and started conversing with everyone around him, smiling and laughing in a very lucid and animated way. As his car inched closer to the pick-up spot, his head quickly dropped, and he went back into his pathetic "victim" routine. He then made his son struggle to communicate with him about getting into the car, and accused him of taking too long in the parking lot. As the car slowly eased into traffic, he actually turned his head and gave us all a quick wink.

I will never know if the son knew he was being duped, that out of duty he "played the game." I think of the relationship this man is missing with his son, his God, and probably his entire family. He could have been "walking" toward the sunset in truth, and building an incredible legacy of love that would be an example for generations to come. Unfortunately, he was providing an example; an example of self-centered complaining and an ungrateful heart.

That is our challenge as we face our last days on earth. Will we become self-centered "victims" in this final test, seeking the gold from others, or will we be the GOLD, reflecting God's love and kindness in self-controlled faithfulness to His will for us?

Will the last day of our life be better than today as we seek to please God?

That is my prayer!

O Father…

keep the wolf far from the doorstep of my heart. Fill me with Your mighty Spirit. I thank You for this precious time of my life. A time when my-world will not see my strengths, for my skills and abilities are waning more everyday. My-world will see Your love and compassion for Your servant. Refine my heart and keep it pure. Let me reflect and magnify Your love and kindness to those around me. Give my-world ears to hear and eyes to see Your character shining through my weakness, for You are the true Gold of not just the "Golden Years," but every year.

Let me one day stand before You and hear You say, "Well done... you allowed my Holy Spirit to control your will and fill your heart with my love, gentleness, kindness and truth." (Gal. 5:22-25)

Claim Your Gold

Application Guide

Engrave your heart:
(Memorize, or simply re-read during the day.)

"...the fruit of the Spirit is
love, joy, peace, patience, kindness, goodness,
faithfulness, gentleness, self-control. *"* -Galatians 5:22-23 -NIV

"If we live in the Spirit, let us ***walk in the Spirit.***
Let us not become conceited,
provoking one another, envying one another." -Galatians 5:25-26

Refine the gold:

When we hear older relatives disrespect someone with unkind, cruel words we sometimes simply say, "Remind me not to get that way." That's a good start, but if we truly want to remember not to fall into negative speech patterns we could re-route our memory to the ***positive***. We could rethink the words of the negative person, and come up with a positive way of saying the same, or similar words.

For practice, rewrite Wolf-Eaten Grandma's words from Chapter Two. Speak in *truth*, but with love, kindness, goodness and gentleness, and with the idea of edifying Little Red. Practice this principle whenever you hear negative, unedifying statements. (Don't be intimidated by the seemingly simplicity of this exercise. It becomes much more difficult as we learn to edit our own negative statements.)

1. WOLF: "Why don't you ever come to see me?"
Positive words:

2. WOLF: "Don't you know I don't like those cookies?"
Positive words:

3. WOLF: "Why are you wearing that hideous red hood? You look like a giant blood clot!"
Positive words:

4. WOLF: "Can't you get a better job? What are you thinking—or are you?"
Positive words:

5. WOLF: "When are you going to get married and settle down?"
Positive words:

7. WOLF: " Where are my slippers?"
Positive words:

*"**Search me**, O God,*
and know my heart; test me and know my anxious thoughts.
*See if there is any **offensive** way in me,*
And lead me in the way everlasting."
-Psalm 139:23-24 (NIV)

Nuggets of wisdom, promises and praise:
(Sing, or simply read as prayerful poetry.)

"Have Thine Own Way, Lord" by Adelaide A Pollard

Have Thine own way, Lord! Have Thine own way!
Thou art the Potter, I am the clay.
Mold me and make me after Thy will,
While I am waiting, yielded and still.

Have Thine own way, Lord! Have Thine own way!
Search me and try me, Master, today!
Whiter than snow, Lord, wash me just now,
While in Thy presence humbly I bow.

Have Thine own way, Lord! Have Thine own way!
Hold o'er my being absolute sway!
Fill with Thy Spirit till all shall see
Christ only, always, living in me!

Chapter 3
Live Out Your Mission

Employ Diligent Perseverance

perseverance, n.- a steady persistence in a course of action, a purpose, a state, especially in spite of difficulties and obstacles.
goal, n.- the result or achievement toward which effort is directed; aim; end.

God has provided countless "backdrops" (conditions of trials, promises and blessings) throughout the history of the world. Each was designed to allow His-Story of compassion, power, and faithfulness to be magnified in the life of an obedient, persevering servant of His.

Some of the settings are remembered because of their importance in the lives of multitudes of people, and over the years these have made wonderful stories that have been repeated numerous times throughout the Christian world. Now, as we are entrenched in a sea of technology we are able to find these miracles of God recorded on videos and DVDs.

The story of Noah's Ark is one example. God set his rainbow in the sky as a promise to coming generations against the "backdrop" of His powerful destruction of the evil, self-centered blackness of the hearts of the inhabitants of His own creation. How could they turn their backs on His great love and provisions for them? How could they laugh in His face at even the slightest hint that they weren't in control of their own lives and destinies?

God provided their generation with one man who lived by God's standards and loved God with all his heart (Genesis 6:9). It was Noah alone who "found grace in the eyes of the LORD" (Genesis 6:8). Noah was God's chosen man because, as the Scriptures report over and over again, he did everything God asked him to do (Genesis 6:22, 7:5).

God gave Noah a very specific goal, and detailed design plans for building the ark that would carry him and his family and all the animals to safety. Noah didn't argue with God's plans! He was a man of faith who fulfilled his purpose of loving his Creator. Because he sought righteousness, God entrusted him with a world-changing goal. A goal for which there was no precedent. The ark would become a symbol of God's saving power.

What faith! What trust! For one hundred and twenty years he was a living illustration to his world, working daily on his God-given goal. All the people came to watch and listen to his words of warning and they walked away laughing. Yet Noah continued—step-by-step, detail-by-detail. Noah persevered in obedience because he focused on God and was undaunted by the multitudes that rejected his message.

The evidence of Noah's love for God was expressed in the faith he had in the plans God had revealed to him, and in the fact that he didn't build in isolation. He reached out to his world every day so that everyone would know of God's plan. He tried to convince them to turn from their self-sufficient pride and seek the purpose for which they had been created. The reason that Noah found grace in God's eyes was because he was submissive to God's authority. He knew what God wanted from him and he didn't cave in to the popular thinking of his day.

Noah's ark could have been built with a lot less irritation. Why did he have to listen to the insults of others? He could have built a large fence to keep out the world and the things they were saying about him—things that put him down and made him appear less intelligent than they. But Noah followed God's plans to the letter. Nowhere in the plan did God tell him to build a fence and isolate himself. On the contrary, God was using Noah's words of warning to give the world one more one-hundred-and-twenty-year chance to proclaim Him as their God. Building a boat in the desert gave Noah the perfect "backdrop" for answering the obvious questions of the day:

"Why?"…

"What are you doing?" And again…

"Why?"

God's compassion and desire for the love of the people overflowed through Noah's lips. And even though Noah was faithful to the task for 120 years, only seven people, besides Noah, were spared the judgment of the flood.

Noah's love for God was reflected to his world—his family. They worked along side Noah day after day and year after year. They saw Noah's passion for pleasing God as he focused on every detail of the plan. They could have worked together on the construction simply because they had been trained to respect their elders. They could have performed their duty to their husband and father because of just that; it was their duty. But Noah loved God with all his heart, and out of the fullness of his heart, his actions and words reflected God's love to his family. They saw the passion, love, and kindness of Noah's words. They were drawn to the Light through the grace and mercy that God showered upon Noah.

Noah's entire family climbed the steps of the ark. They had all been invited by God to "Come into the ark, you and all your household, because I have seen that you are righteous before me in this generation" (Gen. 7:1)

The percentage of the world's population that was allowed to enter the ark of salvation was minute, but it was Noah's whole world! Noah is a pillar of perseverance in the face of adverse criticism. He was not a young man when he finally reached his goal, and yet he was in the prime (primary role) of his life. He is a powerful example to us of what a life that reflects God's love can do to change the course of history.

As we live out our purpose of loving, thanking, and seeking God's will for our lives, He will faithfully set a goal before us and give us the plans to accomplish it. We may never impact the world to the extent that Noah did, but if we are intent on finding His goals for us, and persevere in faith, He will guide our every "step." He is looking for obedient people, young and old, who are willing and eager to get involved with the people that He has placed in their lives. Whenever we are completely focused on seeking God's goal for us in a new day, a new year, or for the rest of our lives, we are in our prime and on our way to becoming golden role models.

I have learned over the years that if I seek my own goals (what *I* think God wants me to do) I spend a lot of time on the wrong path. When I seek His goal for me, and wait for His direction, He faithfully helps me to persevere to its completion.

The writing of this book has been the goal of my heart for the last few years. But was it my goal, or His? Even though God constantly prodded me and bombarded my mind with chapter topics and examples, I rejected the idea of actually sitting down and putting the first word into my computer. Even though I had taught writing skills to my students for many years, who was I to think that I could really write a book? Was there enough to say on the subject of finding "gold" in old age? Day after day I asked the LORD to use me and set a goal for me, and when He did, I kept dragging my feet. Would God bless me in my efforts, or would it be another waste of time? I know that God will not forsake His own, but for some reason months passed and the goal was no closer. (I had run ahead of Him before and didn't want to do it again.) My desire was to be in the center of His plan for me, not running ahead of Him, and not lagging behind.

And then one day He brought to my mind the story of Moses and his goal of getting the Israelites to safety on the other side of the Red Sea. In Exodus 14:15, God basically told Moses that the time for praying was over and it was time to step out in faith and "Go forward." I knew I had come to this place in my spiritual life where I had to stop my fearful, "I can't do it" praying, and just go forward.

In my advancing years, my hopes of pleasing God have been strongly supported as He has guided and encouraged me to persevere and be faithful to the purpose for which He has made me. As each goal is met the LORD faithfully gives me another. He knows me better than I know myself, and He always, "trains my hands" and fits my tasks to His purpose for me.

As time goes by the goals He sets for me will undoubtedly change. My writing may change to simply reading to my grandchildren, or writing encouraging e-mails. Eventually, as my body withers away I will seek less challenging daily goals. The act of smiling, praying, and verbalizing "thank you" to God, and to those He sends my way, may become major achievements.

To whatever extent my physical abilities, or lack there of, allow, I resolve to:

-Always think on good things.

-Stay positive.

-Lovingly edify those around me.

I've watched others go through personal agony at the end of their lives, and yet, because they kept their focus on God's goal for their lives, they showed me, and the rest of their world how to do it right.

The biggest complaint I've heard from retired and aging friends and relatives is the lack of having a meaningful purpose and daily goals. Yet I know from my own experience, and from closely watching my golden role models, that as we ask God for a goal that is pleasing to Him, He faithfully shows us the way.

I pray that we will persevere, especially in the hard times, and that *we* will become God-centered, golden role models, filled with a deep love for others. And on our last day as we "climb" those golden steps, our-world will be watching and will desire to follow in our footsteps, and one day see God's rainbow.

O LORD, Thank You…

for the examples of Noah, Moses, and all my golden role models, as they loved You in difficult situations. Help me to reflect Your love against the conditions of every stage of my life.

I thank You that this time of my life lies before me. Give me goals and opportunities to reflect your love to everyone. For when I am ending my life with a moan, unable to display the energy of my youth, only Your love and care for me can make that happen.

I pray for Your mercy and grace in my life, and in the lives of those in my-world. May they see Your goodness to me and desire it for themselves. Bind me to Your plan in humble perseverance.

May I one day stand before Your glorious rainbow, and hear You say, "Well done...you persevered in My strength, through many difficulties and obstacles (2 Timothy 1:12). *Come in!"*

Claim Your Gold

Application Guide

Engrave your heart:
(Memorize, or simply re-read during the day.)

*"**Come** into the ark, you and all your household, because I have seen
that you are **righteous** before me in this generation."* -Genesis 7:1

*"The path of the **just** is like the shining sun,
That shines even brighter unto the perfect day."*-Proverbs 4:18

Refine the gold:

The effects of aging don't hit us all at once. They creep up on us, and if we're not careful, we slowly, without even knowing it, give in to an ungrateful "victim" mentality. God is not glorified through negative complaining. We must not let an unproductive attitude gain a foothold in our lives. If we are to fulfill our purpose we must obediently seek God's will and meditate on His Word daily to remind ourselves of His clear instructions for ***persevering*** in faith.

1. Read Romans Chapter 12, which outlines goals for faithful Christian living. Notice, especially, verses 9-21, and the list of traits which characterize a Spirit-filled life:
*Verse 9 is a *personal goal.*
* Verses 10-13 explain our *duties to the family of God.*
*Verses 14-16 describe our *duties to others.*

*Verses 17-21 exhort us to remember *God's goal* for us in *dealing with those who consider us enemies.*

2. Look for synonyms for the word *"persevere"* in every verse you read. For example, verse nine says, *"cling,"* and verse 12 says, "*continue steadfastly.*"

3. As you think of your friends and family members throughout the day, remember to pray *steadfastly* for the strength of the Holy Spirit in their lives, as well as your own.

4. Ask God for your *specific* goal for today, this year, and the rest of your life. (Don't just complain that you have no purpose!)

5. Pray for God's guidance to help you know when to *wait on Him,* and when to *go forward.*

6.Thank God, *continually*, for the privilege of having a purpose and goal for your life, and for His mighty power to help you fulfill His desire.

As you research Biblical wisdom this is also an excellent time to get to know your church, and/or your public librarian, if you haven't done so already. If the days come that you can no longer get out and about, you'll have a support system as close as your telephone, and/or your computer. Now is the time to start building relationships that will sustain and support your efforts.

Nuggets of wisdom, promises and praise:
(Sing, or simply read as prayerful poetry.)

"I Know Whom I Have Believed" by Daniel W. Whittle
(based on 2 Timothy 1:12b)

I know not why God's wondrous grace to me He hath made known,
Nor, why, unworthy, Christ in love redeemed me for His own.
But "I know whom I have believed, and am persuaded that He is able
To keep that which I've committed unto Him against that day."

I know not how the Spirit moves, convincing men of sin,
Revealing Jesus through the Word, creating faith in Him.
But "I know whom I have believed, and am persuaded that He is able
To keep that which I've committed unto Him against that day."

I know not when my LORD may come, at night or noonday fair,
Nor if I'll walk the vale with Him, or "meet Him in the air."
But "I know whom I have believed, and am persuaded that He is able
To keep that which I've committed unto Him against that day."

Chapter 4
From Honor to Ashes
Resist Prideful Thinking

honor, n.-1. high respect, as for worth, merit, or rank.
2. high public esteem; fame; glory.
humility, n.- modest opinion of one's own importance or rank.

"Unclean! Unclean!" Miriam's hoarse voice croaked. All the Israelites of her world had to wait while she was paying the penalty for publicly opposing Moses, and calling into question his position as the spokesman for God. For seven days she was afflicted with leprosy and forced to stay with the lepers outside the camp (Numbers 12:14). Her public sin required a public response from the LORD.

Miriam was the first woman in the Bible to be given the honor of the title "prophetess" (Ex. 15:20). In Micah 6:4 she was listed alongside her brothers Moses and Aaron as an integral part of the team that God used to rescue the Israelites from Egyptian bondage. She had used her tongue to sing and praise God in beautiful poetry as the women followed her with "timbrels and with dances" (Ex. 15:20-21). But in the amount of time it took for her to utter a few sentences, Miriam went from the brightest, most honored position ever given to a woman by God, to a pitiful and humbled leper. For she had used her God-honoring tongue to dishonor Moses! She and Aaron verbally attacked Moses! But since her name is mentioned first, and God's punishment fell on her (Num. 12:1-10), she may have been the instigator of this public, verbal abuse.

She was his big sister—the one who helped her parents rescue baby Moses from certain death (Ex. 2:1-10). She was intelligent and well trained in her leadership responsibilities. These skills were just what she needed for her position as co-laborer with Moses and Aaron as they led the Israelites to the Promise Land.

However, the leadership skills she had used so well in her youth to praise and honor God were the same skills that brought her down in her old age. Without seeking God's will and without trusting in Moses' well-documented obedience to God's plan, Miriam, full of pride, expounded her own wisdom. She disparaged Moses—God's chosen mediator between Himself and His people, Israel. She didn't think it was right that Moses had married an Ethiopian. She was aggressive, and she confidently asserted that God had spoken to her and Aaron the way He had spoken to Moses (Numbers 12:2).

God's anger was aroused by Miriam's lack of humility and He answered her (and Aaron's) attack against Moses (Numbers 12:4-9).

Funny how God doesn't focus on Miriam's concerns about Moses' new bride, but goes right to the heart of the matter—Miriam's heart!

Because of his God-proclaimed humility, Moses did not take vengeance on his sister. He didn't even defend himself. He didn't need to, for God was his defender. Miriam and Aaron had attacked His chosen man. They claimed that God had spoken directly to them in the same way that He had spoken directly (face to face) with Moses. They were trying to enhance their "credentials" as they made their case against Moses.

Suddenly, God judged them in His anger! "Who is in charge here? Is it you Miriam? When did your tongue turn from praise to pride? Did you forget the One who gifted you in your youth? Without Me, and My purpose for you, your life is a sham; your wisdom is hollow."

From the outside (I Sam. 16:7), we might say Miriam was nervous about Moses' choice of a foreign wife because of her concern for his leadership responsibilities. Would this marriage negatively affect the people? But we get to go behind the façade. Through the Scriptures (Numbers12:1-15) we get to see what God saw—Miriam's true motive. It appears that jealousy of the influence of Moses was the real cause of their attack. Her words undermined the authority that God had given, face to face, to His humble servant, Moses. She had not been able to transition from her big sister role to her new God-given position of submission to Moses as God's man.

If Miriam had possessed the self-control to make this God-ordained change she would have accepted Moses' new bride with the open arms of a truly Spirit-led person. The whole camp would have witnessed her love as she "walked her talk" of praise and honor. In turn, God would undoubtedly have continued to honor her as He had in her youth. Many times throughout the Scriptures (Proverbs 16:18-20, 18:12, Matthew 23:12) we are taught that when we think ourselves better than we are, God will humble us. But when we humble ourselves, God will exalt us. A person who uses every circumstance of life to honor God can hardly go wrong.

I've witnessed this same self-centered jealousy emerge in even the strongest "Christian" homes. Families that have faithfully followed the letter of the "law" when it came to church attendance and superficial "caring" for others have often ended their relationship with each other because of pride and jealousy. Usually, one member of the group or family will become the self-proclaimed authority of "God's" will for not only the family unit, but also the rest of the outside world. This person does not seek God's desire and will for a given situation, but tries to manipulate other family members through guilt.

Weaker members of the family may even turn their backs on God and flee the home as soon as possible.

One of my closest friends grew up in a family like this. They were required to be in church whenever the doors were open. They knew all the Christian terminology and could talk outsiders, and each other, to death on most any subject. But when it came to peace and unity inside their little family walls, there was none! Eventually the whole family split up. All of them went on to seek their own futures, avoiding the other members as much as possible.

But God had plans for my friend, and through His merciful grace He taught him how to truly submit, in love and in desire. My friend is now in his sixties, and is being used in the lives of everyone in his world. However, that's not the end of the story. Other family members who now need him continue to try to squeeze the life out of him by claiming to speak for God. Even so, this friend is faithful to God's command of honoring and caring for older family members. He and his wife continue to lovingly fill all the needs on a daily basis. But, it is never enough! When he is out helping others, jealousy is aroused, and God's name and "authority" is brought into play.

"God told me you spend too much time helping others!" "Don't you know you're suppose to honor me, and do my will?" And on and on it goes.

I pray for strength and endurance for my friend. And as I watch from the outside, I know he sees God working in his life through this whole experience. And as Moses did, he humbly submits to all of the lessons God has planned for him. His older relative, on the other hand, may never be stricken as Miriam was, but is certainly missing out on God's rewards for faithful servants.

If Miriam had reflected God's love to Moses and his new bride, God might have praised her as He did the Proverbs 31:30-31 woman. "… a woman [men, too] who fears the Lord is to be praised. Give her the reward she has earned and let her works bring her praise at the city gate." Instead, Miriam found herself outside the gates, isolated from her world, humbled by God.

The Scriptures don't record any more self-righteous rebellion on Miriam's part. After seven days of banishment she was reinstated into the camp and eventually died in the wilderness at Kadesh (Num. 20:1).

Our hope would be that she had learned the lesson of humility and was able to humbly and lovingly mentor the next generation. But of course there is the possibility that she turned into the "wolf" of

Little Red's nightmare and created her own negative and complaining isolation booth.

We may never know—but if we are wise we can learn from her prideful mistakes and make it our prayer, while we are able to remember. We will honor God by humbly submitting to Him for the rest of our lives.

O Father, thank You for Your mighty Holy Spirit Who fills my life today. Thank You for refining me and letting me reflect Your love and kindness, Your truth and light. Help me, LORD, to remember that it is Your truth and light that I am to share lovingly with my world. Guard my heart and tongue, and remind me as I reach out to others that I am NOT the Holy Spirit. Expounding my wisdom is not my purpose here on earth. Keep me in Your Word each day, especially during my last days when I forget things so easily. Help me to seek Your wisdom and love before I try to tell someone else how to live.

Help me to honestly search my own heart daily. Do not allow me to overestimate myself and overstep my boundaries.

Let me one day stand before You and hear You say, "Well done… you honored Me with your heart, your tongue, and your life."

Claim Your Gold

Application Guide

Engrave your heart:
(Memorize, or simply re-read during the day.)

*"For I say...to everyone who is among you,
not to **think** of himself more highly than he ought to think,
but to **think** soberly, as God has dealt to each one
a measure of faith."* -Romans 12:3

*"Let nothing be done through selfish ambition or conceit,
but in **lowliness of mind** let each esteem others
better than himself."* -Philippians 2:3

Refine the gold:

God has given each of us an incredible gift, the gift of choice. How we use this gift separates all humanity into two groups. One group of prideful, self-centered "thinkers," sees their way as the best and only way. These people sometimes have the audacity to say they are speaking for God.

The other group has learned the self-control it takes to esteem (honor) others. They truly seek God's will in all things, walking in the power of the Holy Spirit to sincerely edify others through kindness and love, gentleness, patience and peace.

It's no coincidence that "**I**" is at the center of the choices we make that bind us to our motives, and our path. We can choose—

Self**I**sh Pr**I**de or Selfless Hum**I**lity.

1. Ask the LORD to illuminate the motives of your heart in regards to each person in your life.

(Are you humbly honoring each person in an edifying way?)

2. Write down (or think of) the name of one person you have truly honored and esteemed, better than yourself, during the last week, month, or year. (Would God agree?)

3. Record the words you said and the things you did to make this person know that he/she was truly honored. Make it your goal to obey Philippians 2:3 on a daily basis by esteeming others better than yourself.

4. Pray that God will help you honor someone today—in person, on the phone, in a letter or card. (No fool's gold flattery, please!)

5. Miriam's leadership tactics were negative and discouraging as she and Aaron confronted Moses. Consider how they could have honored Moses (and gotten their questions answered) in affirming, edifying and encouraging ways.

Remember, as in Miriam's case, what the LORD wants us to do at one point of our lives may be completely contrary to what He has for us to do today. He asked her (through her parents) to help protect Moses when he was a child. God sent her with Moses and Aaron to lead the Israelites out of Egypt (Micah 6:4). He did not put her in charge! He expected Miriam to put aside her big sister role that was once so needed, and submit to her new role of supportive leadership.

God's Word and plan never change, but as we mature we are used in each other's lives in different capacities. As fathers and mothers we are given the authority over our young children, but as they become mature men and women our position in their lives must change, especially if they are humbly following God's plan for their lives.

Mary had the responsibility to care for Jesus as a child. She faithfully carried out her duty and as He matured to adulthood she knew her role was drastically changed. Imagine God's intervention in her life if she had been conceited about her role. Humility was her path, and it has brought her great honor through all generations.

"... everyone who ***exalts*** *himself will be humbled,*
and he who ***humbles*** *himself will be exalted."* -Luke 18:9-14

Nuggets of wisdom, promises and praise:
(Sing, or simply read as prayerful poetry.)

"Open My Eyes, That I May See" by Clara H. Scott

Open my eyes, that I may see Glimpses of truth Thou hast for me;
Place in my hands the wonderful key, that shall unclasp and set me free.
Silently now I wait for Thee, Ready, my God, Thy will to see;
Open my eyes, illumine me, Spirit divine!

Open my ears, that I may hear Voices of truth Thou sendest clear;
And while the wave notes fall on my ear, everything false will disappear.
Silently now I wait for Thee, Ready, my God, Thy will to see;
Open my ears, illumine me, Spirit divine!

Open my mouth, and let it bear Gladly the warm truth everywhere;
Open my heart, and let me prepare Love with Thy children thus to share.
Silently now I wait for Thee, Ready, my God, Thy will to see;
Open my heart, illumine me, Spirit divine!

Chapter 5
He Left His Throne
Submit to HIS Way

bridge, n.- 1. a structure spanning and
providing passage over a chasm…
v.t.- 2. to join by or as if by a bridge.
example, n.- 1. a pattern or model, as of something,
or someone, to be imitated.

One of the greatest encouragements for all of us is the fact that Christ came to earth as a baby. We can all relate to this starting point. I'm sure He cried out when He was hungry or tired, and yet the Bible tells us He lived a human life without sin. He came to save us and to be our Example.

Throughout His life He endured the limitations of the human form. In Matthew 4:2 we learn that He suffered for 40 days with extreme hunger and yet did not fall to Satan's temptations.

His humanity also caused Him to seek solace from all the demands of the people. He needed rest; He needed a time to be alone with God and encouraged by God.

I won't presume to put words in Christ's mouth, but we can imagine Him moaning (not whining or complaining) with physical exhaustion, and then being comforted and strengthened by His Father.

Christ came to earth as the God-man servant (not victim!) Who bridged the gap between God and mankind. He came as our Savior, and as our Example of a completely righteous life.

The most powerful learning tool from the beginning of time is the use of an example. As an example becomes embedded in the minds of the viewers it establishes not only a pattern, but also the possibilities of life.

When we were kids, all of my neighborhood friends formed a skating and biking club. We thought we were so clever with all the tricks we learned to do (none of which compare to anything that we watch on Extreme Sports today). We hadn't even conceived of the possibilities of flying and flipping through the air (at phenomenal heights and frightening speed) the way the kids of today do. If we had seen the examples of the many possibilities, we would not have been so smug about our minimal efforts.

From the moment we entered this world we tried to mimic every sound and movement of our parents and siblings. Studies of orphans left in unattended nurseries, with little or no social contact, reveal children who do not flourish and thrive. These kids have no reference for the possibilities of life.

There is a great line from a movie that I saw several years ago, that illustrates this concept of viewing an example of what is possible that had previously been considered impossible. The main character of the film found himself in the Alaskan wilderness facing an attack of a large grizzly bear. As the story unfolds it seemed there is no way to conquer the bear and escape. The audience can't imagine a solution. When all hope seems lost he suddenly remembers a picture he had seen at the hunting lodge. The painting dramatically captured an Indian of days gone by killing a larger-than-life bear with a long sharpened pole rigged in a way that would use the bear's own weight and speed of attack, and calculated leverage, to conquer him. When the movie character remembered the illustration he was filled with hope, for he realized that… "What one man can do another man can do!"

If he hadn't seen the possibilities, in the painting, of a "small" man killing an enormous bear, he wouldn't have even begun to know how to try.

Of course, he persevered through the next hour of the show and, with his pocketknife started preparing a long and sturdy, pointed, "spear." He practiced wedging the dull end of the spear into the crevice of a giant rock facing a steep incline. As the background music caused our hearts to pound, and the bear loped furiously down the hill and toward his prey, we could see that the carefully replicated set-up was going to be victorious. The bear was "history" in the hands of someone who knew what was possible, and took the time to prepare. Apart from a lot of hard work and determination, he just needed an example to show him that it could be done.

What wonderful encouragement for us! The Bible gives us a clear portrait of Christ's human life as our example. Christ left His heavenly throne, surrounded by praise and adoration (Rev. 4:2-11), to become our Example and our Savior. In His living we are able to learn the possibilities of earthly life. Through His death and resurrection we have the hope of our own resurrection if we are willing to acknowledge and accept the way of salvation He came to provide.

Luke 22:39-44 tells us that before Christ died in excruciating agony on the cross, He went to the Mount of Olives and prayed, "Father, if it is Your will, take this cup away from Me…" but He didn't end His prayer at that point. He could have! He could have taken on the "victim" role and run away from God's plan for Him.

He could have quickly descended the Mount of Olives—whining, complaining, and cursing God the Father for His unfairness, looking for a deep cave in which to hide. He could have even retreated silently into a neighboring country. He knew the area well! It must have been a looming temptation, and yet Christ continued His passionate prayer to the extent that His human body actually went into a dangerous condition called hematidrosis, the effusion of blood in one's perspiration (through extreme anguish or physical strain, capillaries of the human body can dilate and burst—mingling blood with sweat). Verse 44 says, "His sweat became like great drops of blood falling down to the ground" as He continued to pray in complete submission, "Nevertheless… not My will, but Yours be done."

Through Christ's humanity a final sacrifice and perfect example was provided. He taught us the act of submission to our God-given circumstances in life. Submission and humility allow us to set aside a prideful heart that would tell us we deserve better than what God has planned for us. God always has His best in mind for us, and when we seek Him in obedience and thankfulness He showers us with His abundance.

It has been said that life is 1% circumstances and 99% attitude. The theme of every great book, movie, story or play is almost always based on the positive change in the attitudes, and actions of the main character; the more the attitude changes, the better the outcome of the story. A positive attitude in the midst of overwhelming circumstances seems inhuman! And it is! That's where the promises of God come into play. The Bible is filled with examples of people who either made God-honoring changes in their behavior, or not. If they made the changes it was because of the faith they had that God would help them. That is what Christ knew when He spent hours in prayer. If anyone could have legitimately had pride in Himself, it would have been Jesus, the God-man, the One who lived a perfect life with a brilliant mind, and yet we see Him on His knees before His Father seeking supernatural strength for His human weakness.

Pride in thinking that we are the "know-all" and "end-all" to the purpose of life is the greatest sin against God—and the root of all our sins.

God's first commandment to all the people of the earth is… "You shall have no other gods before Me" (Ex. 20:3). This includes the "god" of ***self***.

There are people who think that because they haven't committed a big sin such as murder, etc., they are "home-free." What they won't allow themselves to realize is that we were created for the purpose of loving, and pleasing God with all our heart, soul and mind (Deut. 6:5). If we neglect to pursue His purpose for us, or worse yet, if we turn our backs on Him, we are placing ourselves above the God of creation and telling Him, with our lives, that our way is better than His.

Many Biblical characters did just that, and God was not pleased! They each had to make a conscience decision to set aside some kind of personal or family problem, and trust God's mercy to help them fulfill their earthly purpose.

Because of their age, Abraham and Sarah practically laughed in God's face when He told them He would build a nation through their old childless bodies, but since they believed God still had a purpose for them, great things happened.

Joseph was the victim of treachery at the hands of his older brothers. He could have succumbed to his circumstances and rejected God's purpose for his life, but he persevered and became part of God's great story.

If the Israelites had not rejected God's plan with many wasted hours of grumbling and complaining, they would have been spared 40 years of wandering aimlessly in the desert, waiting for the disobedient parents to die before the new and trusting generation could enter the Promised Land. The parents' folly became a warning to their children, and the rest of us, that God is not pleased when we grumble against His plan. In First Corinthians 10:6 and 11, Paul teaches us that, "These things happened to them as examples and were written down as warnings for us."

When we willingly put ourselves under His plan, and submit to His purpose, He has promised in His Word to enable us to live—and even flourish and bear fruit (Psalm 92:12-14) in *all* stages and challenges of human life.

"Flourish and bear fruit in old age!"

Did I read that right? What is this "fruit" I'm suppose to bear from my withering limbs, and how will I do it with a "flourish?"

"With God all things are possible" -Matthew 19:26

As life offers the challenge of aging bodies winding down to our final breath, the LORD is able to make even our last feeble day our best day in Him. But we must be willing to accept our "cup" of old age as Christ accepted His "cup"—and be able to pray His prayer,

"...nevertheless, not my will but Yours be done."

He did not come to earth to teach us how to be victims of our circumstances. His example is always before us. He led the way in righteousness, and sometimes silence, as He faced the human pain and humiliation of the cross. Would He expect any less from us as we face the pain and humiliation of an aging "shell"?

We must prepare and not allow ourselves to become ungrateful, complaining, negative victims. We must not give in and give up! We must not become self-centered and self-absorbed. If we choose to follow Christ's example and be that "salt and light" that will draw our world to the "Bridge," then we must learn to handle the coming "days of trouble" (Eccl.12:1-NIV), and moaning, through the strength and power of the Holy Spirit sent to help us glorify the LORD in "Whatever" we do (Col. 3:17).

"Whatever" includes everything... even the moaning of old age. Psalm 90:9 actually warns us that we will end our years with a moan.

It is a given! You more than likely will moan. (I have started moaning already as my knees painfully lift me from a sitting position.) And yet, if you think back through your life there has always been something you could have moaned and complained about. That's where the 99% attitude has made you what you are today, whether negative or positive. That's where the 99% attitude will take you in the future. Actually, the Bible says we are to love God and trust Him with our whole heart. If you do the math, that's 100%!

I wanted to know how to end my years with a moan and still magnify God's love 100% of the time. As I began my research I searched the library and bookstores to see how other people have executed this passage through old age. I was looking for "How to" books, and found many dealing with the physical and financial aspects of facing our 50s, 60s and 70s. Ouch! This was getting too close for comfort! I was looking for something that discussed the duties and responsibilities for *old* people. I mean *really old*! I was looking for a chapter on octogenarians and older.

I did find books on how to provide care for our family members who have been granted a long life, but I didn't find much about how we are to live under the conditions of this blessing. This led me to the conclusion that as long as we are alive, and have any semblance of a healthy mental capacity, we are to pray for the strength of the Holy Spirit to help us replicate Christ-like character in whatever we do (John 14:17; 26; 15:26; 16:13-18; Romans 8:26-27; Hebrews 4:14-16; Jude 20). We are to use our lips in kindness, gentleness and edification of others. We are not to be impatient and selfish, but faithfully, peacefully and joyfully be reaching out to those around us. In all of this, God will help us to flourish!

There is no retirement date when we get permission to kick back and stop reflecting God's love, peace, kindness, joy and the other fruit of the Holy Spirit (Gal. 5:22-25). No one has ever been too old to reflect Christ in some way, and on the other hand, no one has ever been too old to reject God's provisions.

Out of a thankful, trusting heart, God will shine more precious than gold.

O Father…

Fill me with the knowledge of Your will in the matter of my aging body. Let me live today worthy of You, and let me please You in every way 100% of the time. Let me bear fruit in every good work, grow in Your knowledge, and be strengthened with all power according to Your glorious might. May I have great endurance and patience, and joyfully give thanks to You Who has qualified me to share in the inheritance of the saints in the kingdom of Light. Thank You for rescuing me from darkness, and for sending Christ to encourage me, and be my "Bridge" to You.

(Based on Paul's prayer for the Colossians in Colossians 1:9-12)

May I one day stand before You and hear You say, "Well done, you accepted My will for your life and allowed Me to be reflected in your heart even to the end." (Proverbs 17:3)

God's Way

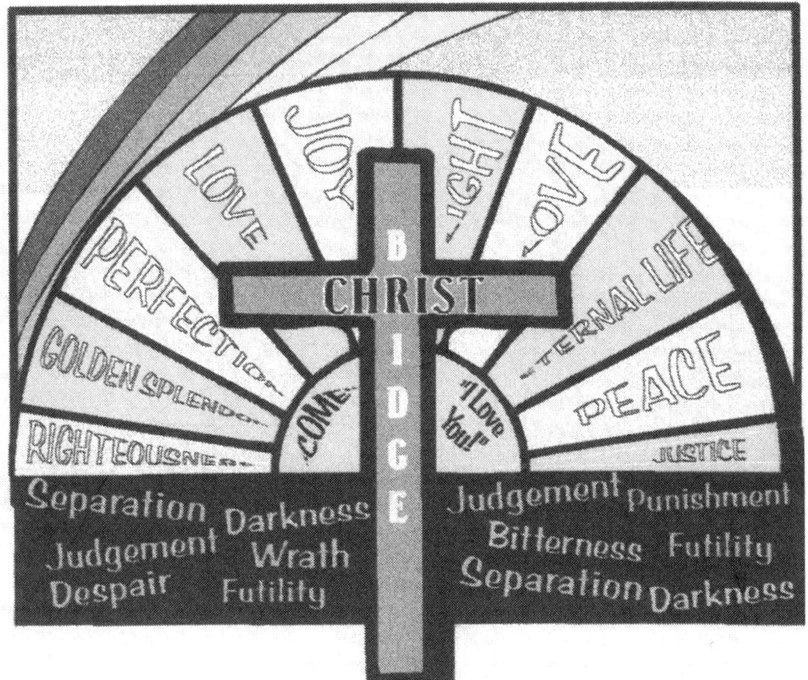

"Jesus said...
'I AM the WAY,
the Truth and the Life.
NO ONE comes to the Father
except through ME'."

-John 14:6

JHM

Claim Your Gold

Application Guide

Engrave your heart:

(Memorize, or simply re-read during the day.)

"And the ***Word*** *became flesh and dwelt among us,*
and we beheld His glory, the glory as of the only begotten of the Father,
full of grace and truth." -John 1:14

"...whoever keeps ***His*** *Word, truly the love of God is perfected in him.*
He who says he abides in ***Him***
ought himself to walk just as ***He*** *walked."* -1 John 2:5-6

"A new commandment I give to you, that you ***love*** *one another;*
as I have loved you, that you also ***love*** *one another.*
By this all will know that you are My disciples,
If you have ***love*** *for one another."* -John 13:34-35

Refine the gold:

Many, if not most, people have learned the art of gracious living—*playing nice*. From childhood up they have been trained by their parents, teachers, Sunday school leaders and, society in general, in the skill of getting along with others. Some of our greatest statesmen, salesmen, etc. have actually developed the ability to control people and manipulate situations through supposed graciousness.

Thankfully, there are also those who truly walk in grace as Christ intended. Webster tells us that God's grace toward us is "unmerited favor and love;" our grace toward others is "the influence or Spirit of God operating in humans," and "a virtue or excellence of divine origin."

We all know people who, in pressure-free environments, exude graciousness. It's not until we view them in stress-filled, out-of-control situations that the truth is known.

Christ walked in grace and truth. When He faced the final hours of His life on earth, the grace, love and mercy He proclaimed were magnified, certified and verified through His continual thoughts and prayers for others. He prayed for the strength and faithfulness of His disciples, and for Christians through all generations. He restored the ear of one who was arresting Him, and asked God to forgive His persecutors. He had asked God to remove this "cup" (death on the cross and separation for God) from Him; then He moved on in the truth of His well-established example. His last day on earth was His **best** day on earth! It capsulated everything He came to do. Paul tells us in Second Corinthians 13:4 that, "He was crucified in weakness, yet He lives by God's power." He is the "Bridge" between sinful man and Holy God, and through His Spirit and example we are empowered to love one another, even unto our last day.

John 13:35 says that there is a way that our world will know if we are true followers of Christ by our love for each other. Not phony, feel-good "grace," but honest love shown through kindness, goodness, gentleness, peace and all the "fruit" of a truly Spirit-filled life. This is not just toward those who return our love, but, as in the case of Jesus, those who despise us and seek to destroy us.

Looking at everyday examples of those around us helps to clarify the intent of God's Word, and gives "feet" to the Gospel.

Jim had invested many years of excellent service in his company. Each of his evaluations was "shinier" than the last. He thrived in the position for which God had trained him. His daily prayer was to reflect Christ's attributes in every situation, without saying a word about what he was doing. He would be an example of love and kindness, peace and patience as he used his wisdom and insights to complete each job.

One day a new employee, Andrew, arrived and changed the office atmosphere of teamwork and encouragement. Negative input became the order of the day. The team had to be prepared to face contrary, undeserved criticism on a daily basis. Many became bitter grumblers, avoiding any situation that might include Andrew.

Jim, however, remembered his father's words that echoed through the years, "You must make a decision to either allow this person to control your reaction to him, or allow the Holy Spirit to control you in an unexpectedly loving and patient way. You always have a choice!" Jim had watched his father "walk his talk" over many years of dealing with contrary and unloving people. He had seen the surprise in their eyes as kind words caught them off guard.

Not every encounter was an immediate success, but seeds of change were being sown, and Jim's dad never had to compromise his integrity. His example was so well etched into Jim's heart that Jim didn't need to think twice about how to respond.

I can't say that Andrew's heart was softened, but I know that God was pleased with Jim's loving attitude toward Andrew. I know that this is not the end of the story, because God had some purpose for Jim's loving life intersecting with Andrew's discontent.

Think of a person who is a truly godly example to you in your world (family, church, etc) whom you have had the privilege to follow through the joys and trials of life. (**Not** one that just looks good on the outside!).

a. Study their godly approach to people.
b. Seek to discover their most helpful and/or favorite Scriptures that have assisted them to become edifying and encouraging.
c. Decide what you will adopt from their example.
d. Ask God to empower you through His Holy Spirit.
e. Thank *God* when people thank you for your faithfulness and obedience to His Word. (Avoid the temptation of pride.)

f. Take time to thank, encourage and pray for all the godly examples in your life.

Is there a person in your world who is destroying his/her testimony to the world as he/she faces this "final exam"?

a. Pray for them daily.
b. Love them even if they don't return your love. (God will!)
c. Pray that God will renew your mind, and protect and shield you from adopting their destructive behavior yourself.
d. Lovingly confront their sin (Gal. 6:1-2).
e. Daily fill your mind with God's Word (Psalm1:1-3).

Evaluate the example you are providing for those around you. Are your words sharp and contrary, causing people to leave your presence as quickly as seems polite, or do others seek your edifying lips? Do you "walk your talk" in all areas?

1. Ask God to reveal the truth about the example you provide for others to follow; is it negative or positive?
2. Pray that the Holy Spirit will help you grow in integrity, matching positive actions to your positive words.
3. View every person on your "path" as a divine privilege and appointment.

*If you don't have the privilege of being close to a truly godly "silver" saint, pray that one will be revealed to you. God may not answer your request in a traditional way, but He will faithfully answer any true seeker's request for insight, wisdom and understanding (Proverbs 2:3-6).

Nuggets of wisdom, promises and praise:
(Sing, or simply read as prayerful poetry.)

"I Want to be Like Jesus" by Thomas O. Chisholm and David Lingstne Ives

I have one deep, supreme desire, that I may be like Jesus.
To this I fervently aspire, that I may be like Jesus.
I want my heart His throne to be, so that a watching world may see
His likeness shining forth in me. I want to be like Jesus.

He spent His life in doing good; I want to be like Jesus.
In lowly paths of service trod; I want to be like Jesus.
He sympathized with hearts distressed;
He spoke the words that cheered and blessed;
He welcomed sinners to His rest. I want to be like Jesus.

Oh, perfect life of Christ, my Lord! I want to be like Jesus.
My recompense and my reward, that I may be like Jesus.
His Spirit fill my hung'ring soul, His power all my life control;
My deepest pray'r, my highest goal, that I may be like Jesus.

Chapter 6

Difficult Days

Prepare for the Coming Trials

difficult, adj.- 1. requiring special effort, skill or planning. 2. fraught with hardship.
trial, n.- affliction or trouble.

King Solomon, the wisest man ever to live, gives us a very gloomy picture of the "difficult days" of old age (Eccl. 12:1). He tells us to serve God now because when we see ourselves in Solomon's imagery of aging in Ecclesiastes 12, we realize that our service to Him will become very limited—not ended as some people would think—but limited. God will always have a purpose for our lives, and even this limited service of a Spirit-filled life will be rewarded (or suffer loss).

As I walk through elder facilities and hospitals with my aging family members, I see the faces and the frail bodies of Ecclesiastes 12. I see Solomon's vivid description of what awaits us, if we are *blessed* with a long life, as he exhorts us to—

Remember now your Creator in the days of your youth, before the difficult days come, and the years draw near when you say, 'I find no pleasure in them': while the sun and the light, the moon and the stars are not darkened, and the clouds do not return after the rain; in the day when the keepers of the house tremble, and the strong men bow down; when the grinders cease because they are few, and those that look through the windows grow dim; when the doors are shut in the streets, and the sound of grinding is low; when one rises up at the sound of a bird, and all the daughters of music are brought low. Also they are afraid of height, and of the terrors in the way; when the almond tree blossoms, and the grasshopper is a burden, and desire fails. For man goes to his eternal home, and the mourners go about the streets. (vv. 1-5)

Solomon's first point in his description is that these days will be difficult and we might say, "I have no pleasure in them." He uses the analogies of a house that is dilapidated and decaying, scenes from nature, and mourners involved in a funeral procession.

In verse two he begins his description by telling us that we can expect to suffer moaning and tears, for he says in his poetic language "the clouds return after the rain." Usually, after it rains the sun comes out—everything looks and smells fresh and glorious. In Solomon's picture it rains and then the clouds return; this is a picture of unending gloom. Our thinking gets cloudy, and the light is dim and depressing. I'm sure when this happens our moaning will increase, but he goes on to tell us there will be more reasons to groan. Our arms, hands, and legs will forsake us as the "keepers of the house tremble and the strong men bow down"(Eccl. 12:3).

If all of this weren't enough, even the simple joy of eating will become a challenge as our teeth (grinders) become fewer. Of course this was written before the dental profession had perfected the art of creating false teeth, but even now some of us will not have dental insurance or funds to avail ourselves of new teeth. If we do, we'll still have to go through the pain of the dental chair, and the process of learning how to use those new "clickers."

In a more positive vein (if you can call this positive!) we won't see or hear much of what is going on in the dental chair because "those that look through the windows (our eyes) grow dim, and all the daughters of music (there go the ears!) are brought low."

As the ears go we'll tend to be left out of more and more conversations because we can't focus on who is speaking. Since we won't hear the flow of the conversation, we won't know when to jump in with something clever to say (that is, if the clouds clear for a moment). Solomon warns us of this in verse four when he says, "the doors (our lips) are shut in the street."

During visits to friends and family members who are now living in retirement homes, I'm very aware of this process. At mealtime I've seen tables of four to six people, who in years past were once animated, but now are eating in silence. After their meal they are taken back to their rooms. Many times this arrangement is easier for the nurses in charge. I asked a nurse if there could be some seating changes in order to find someone with whom they might enjoy sitting. She responded that they do change, but it doesn't make much difference because the older people can't hear each other, and most of them are only focused on their food. When they do speak out, their eyes brighten as they repeat stories from the experiences of their past.

Fortunately, I have discovered that not all care facilities are created equal. When a precious patriarch of our family required around the clock monitoring and care, we spent days visiting care facilities. We would find people eating in silence at one facility, and people smiling toothless grins in the midst of music and laughter at a comparable home just a few miles away. At others, more lucid diners were "bustling" (some with walkers) through the hallways, smiling and greeting one another, as they made their way to a table of friends and uplifting conversations. Each seemed to exhibit some, or many of the signs of old age, and yet most had learned how to find something to enjoy by focusing on each other, and not constantly pointing out all the things they couldn't do any longer.

Our loved one was one of these people. Oh yes, he had his moments of moaning and groaning for his hearing and eyesight were all but gone, and he was dying of cancer, and yet, until his very last day and hour he was positive and encouraging to everyone who crossed his path.

I've also recently watched my uncle go from a high level thinker who loved to articulate his ideas, to a silent fixture in family discussions. He became more and more isolated, and "alone," even in the midst of a noisy crowd, for his speaking skills had been slowly snatched from him. Family members would sit with him and make pleasant "conversation," but at the end of the day we all knew the picture that Solomon had painted for us was living before our very eyes. Was this God's way of preparing us for the funeral that would soon take place? It was a vivid example that is now deeply embedded in my memory, and it reminds me every day, that now is the time to love and serve God, for as I end my days I may be stripped of the ability to even silently breathe a syllable of praise. Hopefully, by that time, my world will be praising Him for me.

As our mental acuity diminishes, our arms and legs give out, and we can hardly see or hear, it's not surprising that we will be "afraid of heights, and of terrors in the way" (Eccl. 12:5). At one time I thought this verse was talking about the older generation still climbing ladders and stairs, and being afraid of falling, or standing nervously at the edge of the Grand Canyon. But now, as I watch my mom and my mother-in-law struggle out of their chairs and down the hallway, I think Solomon was referring to the height of our own body as we stand up. If someone has experienced broken hips as these precious women have, they most likely would be very afraid of another fall—their terror would increase as they try to negotiate familiar (and not so familiar) hallways, sidewalks, restaurants, church aisles, etc.

After reading Solomon's dismal dissertation, we realize why the Bible contains so many verses about honoring our mothers and fathers, and the care of widows, the elderly, and the fatherless. Isaiah 1:17 teaches that the needy are to be protected. To please God we are to, "Learn to do good, seek justice, rebuke the oppressor: defend the fatherless, plead for the widow."

In my earlier years I thought that the word "fatherless" referred to children without parents, or orphans, and it does. But as I have watched the passage of time change family structures, I now see an expanded meaning that could include those older men and women who have lost their mothers and fathers, and are without the emotional (as well as the physical) support of knowing they are still someone's child. During the healthy days of life this is all taken in stride, but as our health, minds, and bodies fail, it would be oh so nice to have the comfort of our mother's love, and our father's care. Even though our children may eventually step forward and become our caretakers during our "difficult days," we will still have to come to terms with the fact that we are fatherless! Fatherless only in an earthly sense! If we have developed a relationship with our heavenly Father, we will never be alone.

God is there, and when we seek Him, even through the darkest days and hours, He will display His unmatchable compassion and support in our lives.

With a personal relationship to our Father in heaven, our days on earth will be transformed, and we will become "new creations," ready to fulfill our purpose "to become like God's Son"(Romans 8:28-29). In order to confirm our trust in God's sovereign control in every circumstance of life we must start now to remove a single three-letter word from our lips and our hearts. The Bible tells us that we are to trust God for He knows our character, and He uses each circumstance of our life to slowly make us more and more like Jesus.

The word that we must reject, when it comes to the motives of God, is "Why?"

"Why, God?"

"Why are You allowing…?"

"Why don't you do things my way?"

If we truly desire to please God and be conformed to the image of His Son, we must put ourselves in the Potter's hands and allow Him to apply the pressure where He knows we need it. I Thessalonians 5:16-18 (NIV) reminds us that we are to "Be joyful always; pray continually; give thanks in all circumstances, for this is God's will for you in Christ Jesus."

Instead of asking, *"Why, God?"* we are to say, *"Thank You, God!"* Not masochistically, thanking God for the pain of the problems, but gratefully, thanking God in each circumstance, because we are 100% convinced that God has our best interests in view, and we know He is with us.

One of my role models told me long ago that the most important thing I could ever hope to take into eternity is my character. He encouraged me to see trials as building blocks to a mature, Christ-like golden character. The more capable we become at handling *loss*, the more prepared we will be. Maturity in Christ will equip us to bear some of the greatest challenges to face the human race—the challenges of aging, and *loss*.

We must prepare in wisdom, but if we continually try to escape the difficult situations we face throughout our lives, we will become like spoiled children—immature, self-centered, seeking our own will and not seeking to glorify God, and not edify others. When we are the ones relegated to supplying comfort and love to ourselves, in trying situations, our resources are limited and inadequate. But when we accept the "why" of each situation as a way of transforming our lives, and we thank God in them, God becomes the source of our peace. He will never leave us or forsake us. And as we seek His will in every problem-solving situation, He grows us, trains us for more useful service, comforts us, and gives us a larger capacity for glorifying His Name.

Many, however, simply wish to escape all problem solving. When bad things happen they merely shift the blame to others, or use TV, radio, video games and the Internet, alcohol, drugs and overeating, constant overtime at work, etc., as distractions to avoid having to deal with growing a strong model character. Many in our society are on the side of these so-called "victims." Why build character when you can hide out, coast, and then complain about how unfair life is?

I've seen it over and over again as a teacher. Students who need constant, positive parenting are many times left to raise themselves as family members are too "busy" avoiding involvement that would take some consistent effort on their part. Complaining and blame shifting are almost guaranteed when parent conference time rolls around. These are the parents who are training their own future caregivers in the art of avoidance and immature character qualities.

On the other hand, maturity in Christ gives us a better handle on the challenges we must face through out our lives, and especially the dramatic changes in our sunset years. When we agree to the process of submission to building a Christ-like character, God faithfully allows us to experience the meaning of His overwhelming love, hope and comfort, and through the process our Father's Name is glorified.

In 2 Corinthians 7:5-6 Paul tells us, "...our bodies had no rest, but we were troubled on every side. Nevertheless God, who comforts the downcast, comforted us by the coming of Titus…." When Paul needed hope, God sent comfort and encouragement through the presence of Titus, and Paul rejoiced exceedingly (7:13).

Imagine that reunion, filled with needed comfort and joy. But my mind is now remembering the scene in Grandma's bedroom as Little Red tried to bring comfort, love and encouragement to her wolf-eaten Granny. Self-centered immaturity would not allow Red's gracious comfort to take hold in Grandma's heart. Whereas with Paul's Christ-like character, God's comforting Hand was received with overwhelming joy.

Those whose eyes are watching us will assess even our reaction to gestures of kindness and love. Imagine Titus' thoughts if Paul had reacted to his coming with angry accusations and indifference, as Grandma reacted to Little Red Riding Hood. Hope would have been dashed, and God's Name tarnished as His comfort was belittled and rejected.

O Father...

You are my Father! You love me with more compassion and care than any human has ever loved me. You knew me, and my every need, before the foundation of the earth (John 17:24*). I pray that You will glorify and magnify Yourself in my weakness* (2 Corinthians 12:9), *and when I groan, as Your Word says I will, let me remember to bring my groaning to You. Your Word teaches me to seek, ask, and knock, and I know from past experience that You always give me just what I* need, *just when I need it. Hold my heart, and my tongue, in Your Hands that I may never grumble against Your provision.*

Fill me, for I know I can do nothing of eternal value in my own "strength." Keep me faithfully submitted to this "cup" You have assigned to me, and let only Your will prevail. Shine through my weakness in a way that You could never shine through me while I *had "control" of my life. Let me praise Your Holy Name and thank You in ALL things. Hide me, LORD, under the shadow of Your loving wings* (Palms 17:8) *for Your loving kindness is better than life.*

Let me one day stand before You and hear You say, "Well done... come to Me, and let Me love you more."

Claim Your Gold

Application Guide

Engrave your heart:
(Memorize, or simply re-read during the day.)

*"**The LORD** is the everlasting God, the Creator of the ends of the earth.*
*He will not grow tired or weary and His **understanding** no one can fathom.*
*He gives **strength** to the weary and increases the **power** of the weak..."*
-Isaiah 40:28-29 (NIV)

"In this you greatly rejoice, though now for a little while,
if need be, you have been grieved by various trials,
*that the **genuineness of your faith** being much more precious than **gold**, ...*
may be found to praise, honor and glory at the revelation of Jesus Christ,
*whom having not seen you **love**."* -1 Peter 1:6-8

Refine the gold:

God understands our needs and motives even better than we do. We are swayed by our wants and our desires. Through various trials God refines and purifies our desires to reflect His desires. If we are found *genuine* in our faith, God is faithful to fill us with "an inexpressible and glorious joy…" (1 Peter 1:8).

As our time on earth gets shorter and shorter it is incredibly important that "as we have opportunity let us do good to all…" (Galatians 6:10).

Throughout history (*His story*), great inventions have come along that have allowed mankind access to God's truth. Highways were built through the heart of Israel and to the four corners of the then known world that allowed Christ's early followers to carry the gospel in many directions. Ships were built and the Word sailed the seas to the far off lands of the Mediterranean, through Paul and those who traveled with him. The printing press, radio, telephone, television and computer have all become opportunities to praise, honor and glorify Jesus Christ. Of course, like anything else their use is determined by the motives of the users.

All of us have used these inventions in one way or another. Some of us have already tapped the power of these forms of communication to magnify God's precious name. God has chosen to put us in this age of technology. (We could have been born in a different time and place.) He has told us to use the opportunities that we have to do good.

Now, even from our own homes we can penetrate the far corners of the earth, with God's hope and light, simply by the click of a little mouse. Modern missionaries are encouraged by e-mail from caring supporters. Grandkids and other family members look forward to loving, encouraging words sent in a way, like e-mail, that will enable them to quickly respond, thus providing a convenient channel to speak into someone's life.

Do not pass up this most powerful opportunity. Not only will it allow you to be in touch with your-world, it will also be a "window to the world" when the difficult days loom on your doorstep, for it will allow you to enter libraries, newspapers, radio and television stations, etc. to view all their resources. Bible software will make reading God's word possible as dimming eyes prevail, for every year that passes a larger font can be used. What a blessing lies before us!

But **now** is the time to prepare!

Many of us have already gone through the "dummy" stage with our computer. If you are one of those who have conquered the basics of e-mail, the internet, and basic document creation…Congratulations! Your action plan is to help someone else learn those skills—a great time to display all the "fruit" of the Spirit, especially patience!

If you haven't tackled the computer yet DON'T SKIP THIS SECTION!

Remember, if you're not going forward while everyone else is, you are not just standing still; you are essentially going backward.

Soon enough you will be left out of the "loop," with muffled hearing and dimming eyes. Why would you put yourself at another disadvantage when with a little perseverance you could continue to participate?

1. Get access to a computer.
   a. Buy one from a source that gives lessons. #1 choice!
   b. Use the one in the public library.
   c. Look for hand-me-downs when friends or family buy new.
   d. Sign-up to take a computer class at your local computer store, through college, etc.
   e. Persuade a friend or family member to teach you on their computer.
   f. Be creative in your pursuit!
   g. Take beginning classes **several times** if you need to.
   h. Learn to enlarge fonts, write letters, and make address labels.
2. Review "*perseverance*" verses on a daily basis. OBEY them!
3. Get hooked-up to the Internet. (There are now ways of using the Internet without using a computer.)
4. Ask your grandkids, nieces, nephews, etc. to e-mail you for practice. (A great way to start a deeper relationship, and share the genuineness of your faith.)
5. Have fun! (It takes awhile to get to that point, but it will happen.)
6. **DON'T GIVE-UP! DON'T MAKE EXCUSES!** Thank God for every step you take. Everything is from His Hand. Pray that God will guide you as you seek new ways to glorify His Holy Name using all your new skills.

Of course, learning to use the computer is **not** a spiritual requirement. It is just a tool. As the invention of the printing press helped put the Bible into the hands of many, Bible software will make it even more accessible, especially for those of us who will eventually need large print. New technology is being created every day by aging Baby Boomers, with their own needs in mind. Their physical challenges will match the challenges that Solomon described so long ago. Some things don't change, but God has placed us in a world of new opportunities. Don't let them slip away!

"I will ***sing*** *of the mercies of the LORD forever,*
With my mouth (or whatever tool You give me) *will I* ***make known***
Your faithfulness to all generations." -Psalm 89:1

Nuggets of wisdom, promises and praise:
(Sing, or simply read as prayerful poetry.)

"Higher Ground" by Johnson Oatman, Jr.

I'm pressing on the upward way,
New heights I'm gaining every day—
Still praying as I'm onward bound,
"Lord, plant my feet on higher ground."

Lord, lift me up and let me stand
By faith on heaven's table land;
A higher plane than I have found—
Lord, plant my feet on higher ground.

I want to scale the utmost height
And catch a gleam of glory bright;
But still I'll pray till heav'n I've found,
"Lord, lead me on to higher ground."

Lord, lift me up and let me stand
By faith on heaven's table land;
A higher plane than I have found—
Lord, plant my feet on higher ground.

Chapter 7
Remember!
Retain God's Commands and Promises

remember, v.- 1. to retain in the mind;
remain aware of.
2. to exercise the faculty of memory
faithful, adj.- reliable, trusted, believed.

I love the way the LORD gives us the impossible to do, because when we submit and do it, we know for certain that the praise and glory belongs to God alone.

I don't know about you, but my memory is becoming very "slippery"! I have to make lists of things to remember, and then I have to write notes to remind myself to read the lists. My only comfort is that my friends and older family members are experiencing the same thing. And yet, God tells us over and over again in the Bible to "remember" (Psalm 42:4), "remember" (Psalm 63:6), "remember"(Eccl. 12:1), because in remembering His goodness and the power of His love, we find our peace and joy for living.

But how do we do that?

I'm reminded of a story our Bible Study teacher, Warren Currie (President/CEO of the Union Rescue Mission in L.A.), illuminated for us several years ago. We were studying this very topic of God's provision for those He loves. The point of the study was to figure out why we tend to doubt His care for us even after watching His mighty Hand at work in our lives.

Warren led us first to Exodus and all the miracles God performed in order to bring His children, the Israelites, into the Promised Land. These people were eyewitnesses to the most incredible, awesome miracles of God. He showed them His power and love for them through the many curses He put on their enemy and taskmaster, Egypt. He parted the Red Sea, the manna rained down for 40 years, they always had water, their clothes never wore out, etc. Their job was simply to follow Him, trust Him, and do what He asked them to do. He did everything for them either directly or through His humble servant, Moses. In the beginning they praised His goodness to them (Miriam and Moses danced in praise after the parting of the Red Sea). They sang, gave thanks, and glorified His Name. But then—they forgot! They didn't have the food they wanted, and the water they wanted and needed was not immediately available to them the minute they desired it (Ex. 15:23-16:3), so the people slandered Moses and God (Numbers 20:5). (And we think we live in the instant-gratification generation. Human nature is still the same!) They accused Moses of bringing them to the desert to die and asked him if there weren't enough graves in Egypt (Ex. 14:11).

They didn't "get it"—they forgot!

In their immediate panic and need for water, they completely forgot their thankfulness to God for allowing them to view His mighty miracles. Did they really think that God would take them this far and then forsake them? They had God with them—leading them—and they forgot!

We have God's Word at our fingertips and we forget that He promised He would *never* leave us, or forsake us (Deut. 31:6). Why do we keep forgetting, doubting, and even sometimes slandering God with our grumbling—when *He* is our only hope?

That was the question before us as we "walked" through some New Testament passages. We rediscovered a favorite flannel-graph story from our earlier years in Sunday School. The story of the feeding of the 5,000 (Mark 6:32-52) is one of those stories that is repeated—again and again—to kids of all ages. We were feeling a little insulted when our teacher suggested that we needed to hear it one more time at our advanced ages. We sat through the story, nodding, and even quoting some of the words… "five loaves and two fish"… "about 5000 men plus women and children"… "they all ate and were filled." Still a great story!

With God, nothing is impossible. Yes, that's true, but that was not his point in bringing us to this passage. As we read on we remembered that Christ told His twelve disciples to pick up the leftovers. In obedience, each man took their small basket and filled it with the fragments of a mighty miracle. These crumbs were exactly enough to fill all 12 baskets.

As soon as the baskets were full, Christ told His disciples to get into the boat and go before Him to the other side. With the baskets in their hands they jumped into the boat and pushed off. How do you man a boat with a basket in your hands? You don't! We can almost see them putting their small God-filled baskets between their feet for safety. (At least they all knew where their next meal could be found.)

This trip was undoubtedly meant to be a test of their faith. The test began as the wind pushed them further and further away from shore. They were straining at the oars, fighting the battle of another storm (Christ had remained on shore, waiting and praying).

What were these sailors thinking? Did they doubt His love and purpose for them? Did the tossing of their little boat and the windswept waves cause their memories to fail? Just two chapters earlier, Christ had been with them in a boat that began to fill with water during a great windstorm. Christ was asleep in the stern, humanly exhausted from a long day of teaching. When they finally roused Him their first words echoed the words of the Israelites in the desert, "Teacher, do You not care that we are perishing?" (Mark 4:38). In the time it took for Christ to speak just three small words, "Peace, be still!"… the water was again calm. Instantly, which was contrary to anything they had experienced before in all their years as fishermen, the waters were as smooth as glass (Mark 4:39).

In the midst of this new storm, were they thinking what they had verbalized earlier,… "Did He send us here to die?" Did they forget those baskets at their feet, and the supernatural power that Jesus had displayed to create enough food to feed thousands of people? Did they forget His words of, "Peace be still?" And who was that walking on the waves? "It must be a ghost, a phantom, an apparition of our minds created by our fear and fatigue."

They didn't "get it"—they forgot!

They kept straining at the oars—crying out in terror (Mark 6:49-50). With all the evidence they had of His faithfulness their first words should have been, "Jesus, we need You! You have the power to give us peace." Why didn't they?

Why don't we? We have "baskets" of answered prayers—and still we doubt!

As we read to the end of the disciples' story of walking for three years with Jesus, we know that this test wasn't the last test of faith they failed. In their fear and panic during Christ's arrest and crucifixion they all deserted Him. Even Peter—the most passionate, impetuous, and seemingly courageous one of all—fulfilled Jesus' prediction—he denied Him three times (John 18:15-27).

Didn't they remember anything from being with God, in the form of Jesus Christ, for the last three years? If all His personal mentoring and unmatchable miracles didn't bring them to complete faithfulness and trust in Him, what is our hope to remain faithful when we are tested during our days of difficulty?

O Lord,

I know Your Word says that the righteous will still produce fruit in their old age. In Galatians 5:22 You taught us the meaning of "fruit." Nine choice qualities of "fruit" are listed including: love, joy, peace, kindness, goodness, gentleness, patience, self-control and faithfulness.

The one major quality that seems to have eluded the disciples was "faithfulness." If those who actually walked with You could not remember to be faithful, how will I?

Teach me, Father. My greatest desire is to one-day step into Your presence, to see You smile at me and hear You say, "Well done... you zealously, and wholeheartedly trusted Me until this very day" (Psalm 119:2,34).

Claim Your Gold

Application Guide

Engrave your heart:
(Memorize, or simply re-read during the day.)

"Be careful, and watch yourselves closely
so that you ***do not forget*** *the things your eyes have seen*
or let them slip from your heart as long as you live.
Teach them to your children and to their children after them.
Remember*..."* -Deuteronomy 4:9-10 -NIV

"I will ***remember*** *the years of the right Hand of the Most High.*
I will ***remember*** *the works of the LORD;*
Surely I will ***remember*** *Your wonders of old.*
I will also meditate on all Your work, And talk of your deeds."
-Psalm 77:10-12 –KJV

Refine the gold:

When God tells us to "Be careful, and watch yourselves closely so you do not forget the things your eyes have seen... as long as you live," we realize that He is asking us to be responsible for remembering all His blessings in our lives, and the lives of others. He will not forsake us! If we propose in our hearts to truly obey Him, His Holy Spirit will empower us to be faithful, and there will be a "harvest" of "fruit" in our lives. A harvest of loving kindness, peace and faithfulness saturated with joy.

God gives us a memory tool within the verse of admonition to "remember," He tells us to "**teach**." God knows what works! He created our brains and our capacity for remembering. He knows that when we learn a concept well enough to teach it to someone else, *we* will remember much more than our "student." Dedicated preachers admit this from the pulpit. As they search the Scriptures for main ideas that can be capsulated into a 30-45 minute sermon, they spend hours researching and taking notes that will help them synthesize the meaning to make it clear. In the process, their spiritual understanding grows at a faster rate than the growth of those who simply listen.

As with everything else, none of us are exactly the same. And yet, we are much more alike (about 97% the same) than we are different (3%).

God commands us in His Word to use many, if not all of the memory techniques that He has given us, to remember and apply His Word. He tells us to "***read, hear, meditate, sing, teach, write, see, do***..." Educational studies validate these methods, and even try to quantify their effectiveness when it comes to retaining information.

In order to please God we must know, and ***remember***, what pleases Him. If we read His Word, only once, we tend to remember only about 10% of the content; hearing God's truth raises our retention to 20%; summarizing what we've read and/or heard jumps retention to about 70%. As was stated earlier, once we translate our learning into action, we tend to retain nearly 80% of what God's Word is trying to teach us.

Aside from the invention of the computer, one of the most helpful inventions of the 20th century have been "Post-it" Notes. What a great idea! I stick them everywhere when I'm trying to remember something. I put them on the inside of the front door to remind me of things I need to do before I leave the house. I put them on the dashboard of my car to jog my memory after work. I use them in my checkbook, phone book, and every other book that has meaning for me.

This year as I started reading through my well-marked Study Bible, I decided to jot key words that *capsulate* the meaning of each day's reading on Post-its, and stick them to the edge of each page. My Study Bible has become a conversation piece in our home. With 260 sticky notes (so far) lining the edge of the pages, my family laughs at me, and asks how I can ever find anything if I need it. It's amazing, but when I need a verse of encouragement for a pressing situation, I always seem to find the note I want, or the note I need.

Every month or so, I set aside time to re-read all the notes. Summarizing concepts from God's Word, on a daily basis, has helped me profoundly to remember what pleases my Heavenly Father as I interact with His other children each day.

Next year, when I start a new Study Bible, I plan to use multi-colored "stickies" to mark different character qualities that are pleasing to God. I can't wait to hear my family's reaction to that.

"***Read, hear, meditate, sing, teach, write, see, do***..." are all action verbs. God has spelled out our "homework assignments" very clearly. Some would say, "I don't know what He wants me to do." To those people I say, start with the obvious. When the Scriptures say "*read*," READ! If His Word says, "*Give thanks*," **Thank Him**!

1. Every time you read and meditate on God's Word:
   a. Underline the action verbs ***("read, hear, meditate, sing, teach, write, see, do, thank, etc.")***.
   b. Apply, not just God's teachings, but also His methods. If He says, "*hear*" then read the passage again aloud. If He says "*sing,*" sing a hymn of thanksgiving, or read one of the Psalms out loud.
   c. Make it a daily goal to share ("*teach*") what you've read, in casual, loving conversation during the day.
   d. Always try to find a way to "*apply*" what you've read on the day you read it, and continue its application.

2. To help yourself remember the content of a passage, write it and ***reconfigure*** the position of some of the words to help your mind grasp it, and retain its meaning. (This is for remembering content, not for memorizing, and reciting the actual words of Scripture.)

EXAMPLE #1: Write character-building words ***Alphabetically*** as in:

"The fruit of the Spirit is
F*aithfulness,*
G*entleness,* ***G****oodness,*
J*oy,*
K*indness,*
L*ove,*
P*atience,* ***P****eace,*
S*elf-control.*
-Galatians 5:22-23

EXAMPLE #2: Write words in groups, and/or visually separated, with different fonts and sizes—Be creative! (Use those computer skills you've developed.)
"The fruit of the Spirit is
love, joy, peace,
KINDNESS, GOODNESS, GENTLENESS,
patience, self-control, faithfulness."
-Galatians 5:22-23

(Many Christians have read these verses repeatedly, but cannot recite all ***nine*** attitudes of the "fruit" of the Spirit. We ***must*** be sure of our goal, before we can reach it.)

3. If you have a personal relationship with Jesus Christ, think about your life before you became a Christian. How did you come to know you needed Him in your life? How has He changed you? What are you doing to please Him now?

4. Write-out your own story of how Christ has transformed your life. Add to it each year, as you grow in Him. (Writing it out will help you recall the details, and make it easier to relay when you share it with someone.)

5. Pray that God will lead you to someone (maybe a grandchild, a neighbor, a friend), who is interested, and excited, about hearing your story. ***Tell*** your story; don't read it!

6. Thank God for every opportunity He brings into your life to share your testimony of His love for you.

7. Sing your praise to Him.

Nuggets of Wisdom, Promises and Praise:
(Sing, or simply read as prayerful poetry.)

"Tell Me the Old, Old Story" by A. Catherine Hankey

Tell me the old, old story Of unseen things above,
Of Jesus and His glory, Of Jesus and His love.
Tell me the story simply, As to a little child,
For I am weak and weary, And helpless and defiled.
Refrain:
Tell me the old, old story, Tell me the old, old story,
Tell me the old, old story Of Jesus and His love.

Tell me the story slowly, That I may take it in—
That wonderful redemption, God's remedy for sin.
Tell me the story often, For I forget so soon;
The early dew of morning Has passed away at noon.
Refrain

Tell me the same old story When you have cause to fear
That this world's empty glory Is costing me too dear.
Tell me the story always, If you would really be,
In any time of trouble, A comforter to me.
Refrain

Chapter 8

180°... 24/7

Seek God's Power for an Invigorated Life

change, v.- 1. to make different.
2. to transform.
continual, adj.- happening without interruption
or cessation.

Life on earth is so much like life in a classroom. There are always lessons to be learned.

One of the greatest connections we have with one another is the fact that all of us have been created for change. We all have joined the human life cycle. Since Adam, none of us came to earth as a mature being with a fully developed sense of life, and how it is to be maximized for the Creator's pleasure and purpose. Every one of us will cycle through incredible physical changes from the first day we arrived on this planet until our last, but it's the inward changes that will determine our future in the light of God's plan.

We've all been in many types of "classrooms" (or learning situations) during the span of our lives. From our very first day, the "classroom" of our mother's arms taught us much. If she was there for us, we learned to trust. If we were left with minimal support, we learned other lessons. Whether we like it or not, we are all moving through the "classrooms" of life. Every phase and situation is a learning opportunity. Some of us will be quick to learn and move on. Some, however, will be unwilling to submit to the cycle that leads to maturity, and will constantly have to redo their "lessons." Their bodies will move to the next stage of the cycle automatically, but maturity in the purpose for which they were created will elude them. Life will become a merry-go-round of ups and downs, going nowhere except to the end of the ride.

I picture little kids enjoying the carousel for the first time; how excited they are. The next picture that comes to my mind is a scene of the same "kids" 80 years later, trapped on the same ride, going nowhere, and refusing to get off. They are all afraid of the new "classrooms," and lessons that might face them if they leave the safety, boredom, and ineffectiveness of their futile lives. God did not create us for futility. He gave each of us (no matter our mental and/or physical capacity) incredible value. And He has promised us, in the Bible, that He will teach us to maximize that value for His glory.

As a teacher, it excites me to learn God's teaching methods, and then work out ways of implementing His "best practices" with my own students. Whether we realize it or not, we are all teachers. We all have "students" with very keen eyes learning life lessons from us: our family members, neighbors, our fellow workers and boss, and our friends. Will we teach positive, edifying lessons that will lead to maturity; or will our "students" be carousel riders, unable to accept responsibility for the outcome of their lives?

Jesus' teaching style on earth was always tempered to fit the learning style of His "students." Because He completely understood the capacity of each of His students and what was in their hearts and minds, He was able to come alongside them, and speak to them, using practical, everyday visual aids and stories that would help them (and us) to see the deeper meaning and purpose that He had for them. He spoke to them in parables; using their agrarian surroundings as His "classroom" to teach them spiritual truth, how to pray, and how to serve each other with humble hands. He talked about the mustard seeds, lost sheep, workers in a vineyard, etc. He drew word pictures for them using concepts that they knew well. They were amazed with His wisdom and mighty works (Matt 13:54).

Many of His true followers had been waiting all their lives for the fulfillment of the Scriptures (Isaiah) concerning Christ's arrival, and His activities on earth. Many abandoned their old lives to follow Him (Luke 9:23-24, Romans 12:2). He came to point the way to the exit of life's merry-go-round. He *is* the Way!

Through His Word He teaches us:

"And do not be conformed to this world, but be transformed by the ***renewing of your mind****, that you may prove what is that good and acceptable, and perfect will of God."*-Romans 12:2

This was the lesson He was teaching His disciples as they agreed to follow Him through Israel, and be His students. In the process of putting themselves in Christ's circle of followers, their lives changed direction 180°. They were on a new path—becoming fishers of men instead of fish (Matt. 4:19). But how do you take a fisherman, a tax collector, a doubter, a zealot, and all the others, and teach them what they needed to know to successfully do their new job? Christ had three years to accomplish this feat.

Christ had created them (Eph. 2:10), and their capacity for learning. He knew them inside out! His first goal was to teach them about themselves; their weaknesses and the limitations of their personalities. He actually chose them because they were lowly, uneducated Galileans, unqualified, in the world's eyes, as leadership material.

He began by showing them they had a need for something more than just their own strengths and insights. Peter was aggressive and bold, but his mouth was foot-shaped. He habitually jumped into conversations, and situations, before thinking them through. Thomas was a skeptic and doubter, and Matthew was a hated tax collector. The rest of the twelve were also filled with tremendous human frailties and flaws. Christ would mold them to become willing messengers of God.

His first lesson was to bring them to the place where they submitted to His plan for them. (This is the first lesson we all face.) They thought He had come to set up His kingdom on earth, and they were drawn to Him by their desire to help Him. They wanted to be part of the new government. They soon discovered that if they wanted to remain in His circle they had to change their perspective. He was looking to make disciples resulting in eternal life with God. They were looking for solutions to their immediate, temporal needs.

Passionate Peter had made a self-sacrificing vow to Jesus, "I will lay down my life for your sake!" (John 13:37). But Christ knew His student so well. He knew that the words on his lips did *not* reflect the truth in his heart. Peter wanted to make the 180-degree commitment, and in his own strength he managed it part of the time. But, when Peter's "final exam" came during Christ's arrest, the words he had spoken were forgotten. He panicked! He didn't remember even one of the supernatural things he had witnessed during the last three years with his Teacher, Jesus. He had been with Jesus as He calmed the storms, walked on the water, and fed the 5,000 with a few fish and loaves. He had just spent three incredible years witnessing Christ's character and power, and yet, he denied that he ever knew Him (John 18:15-27).

Peter's commitment was compromised! He couldn't pass the test, seven days a week, 24 hours a day. Jesus had told him that when the hour of His betrayal by Judas arrived, Peter would also betray Him by denying he knew Him three different times before the night had ended and the rooster crowed. Of course Christ was right. Peter glued himself to the scene of the action as Christ was arrested and taken to a midnight, hurry-up trial. But as the onlookers pointed to him as a friend of the accused, Peter denied any connection. As the rooster crowed, Peter's memory suddenly returned. His "grades" were in! He had failed his test—three times—just as Jesus had predicted. And as most true and passionate students do when they fail, "he went out and wept bitterly" (Luke 22:62).

The clincher to this whole story is a technique that teachers have used since time began. It's called the "Teacher Look." Luke 22:60-

61 describes it completely… "While he (Peter) was still speaking (denying that he knew Christ), the rooster crowed, and the LORD turned and looked at Peter." There it is! The "Look"! Peter's heart was pierced, and finally humbled.

NOW… he could be changed, and used in a mighty way.

Once we humble ourselves, and realize that God's plan is in place and operating 24–7, we can choose to submit to His leadership and purpose for our lives. On the other hand, we can choose to continue in our disillusionment, and deny the existence of the spiritual dimension of the kingdom of God. If that is the choice of our heart, we will always be an "outsider," even if our lips acknowledge His kingdom and we pretend to be a part of it if only when it is convenient and expedient.

Throughout our lives most of us have heard those familiar words, "You can do it! You can do it! Anything you want to do—if you want it badly enough and work hard—you can do it!"

These words are meant to be words of encouragement. We've probably all said them to someone else at one time or another.

When we hear these words, or say them ourselves, we need to remember to add the balance of God's will to the statement. We must not confuse people into prideful thinking that excludes what God has planned for them. We must restate our encouragement and point our "students" to God's excellent plan for their lives. Better words would be, "God has the perfect plan for your life. Seek Him, and He will not only show you His plan, He will train you, and prepare you to excel." (based on Eph. 2:10)

In Matthew 14:28-31, Christ encouraged Peter. He told Peter he could walk on the water if he desired. He basically said, "Come, you can do it!" This was in God's plan for Peter. He took the desire and passion in Peter's heart, and prepared a lesson of trust. But Peter forgot to keep his eyes on Jesus. He let the waves distract him. In his humanness he lost his focus, was filled with fear, and began to sink. In his desperation he regained his focal point, for he knew he couldn't save himself; he cried out to the Lord.

When we hear, "You can do anything if you work hard enough," we must check the motives of our hearts. Will we bc prideful and use our heart, soul, strength, and mind to gain temporary profit and self-edification? Or, will we keep our focus and seek to walk in a way that would point others to God's heavenly kingdom? Walking—with our focus on God—is a tricky balancing act. We have a good mind, our body is energetic and filled with strength, and in our heart we desire to do good. Our lips proclaim our love for Him, but as we jump, or are thrown into the boisterous waves, the true test begins. Can we maintain the balance so crucially needed to glorify God, and *not* ourselves? Can we make a commitment of 180-degree change, on a 24-hours-a-day-seven-days-a-week basis?

One of my favorite lessons that I teach at the beginning of every year combines drawing techniques, and physiology. The students are each given a small mirror in which to view their own face. As we discuss the shape and placement of facial features, the students record their findings in the form of a self-portrait. The kids love this lesson! Once they get passed their embarrassment, they began to discuss their facial strengths and weaknesses with each other.

As we move to the next step of drawing each other, I can see the empathy they show for one and other's weaknesses, for they have already seen their own.

This compassion is nice while it lasts, but it never endures 24/7. At the first sign of trouble on the playground, physical defects are being loudly insulted in hurtful, unimaginable ways.

We always hope that kids will mature, and outgrow their childish behavior. But all of us know someone who has grown an adult body, yet still harbors the "playground" mentality when trials arise, because they simply won't get off the merry-go-round of familiar behavior. It's easier to continue to go 360-degrees, round and round, always back to the same starting point, than it is to seek the exit sign, refocus, and make a 180-degree change in attitudes and behavior.

For all of you clock (or calendar) watchers out there, we know that our time on earth is quickly coming to an end. When I celebrated my 60th birthday, I did the math and realized that my life was two-thirds over. And that was assuming I would live to see my 90th birthday. I don't have that guarantee. Actually, insurance timetables indicate that my chances of dying in my 70s is much more likely than living to 90. If that is the case, I must carefully plan my next few years. Do I want to get sucked into the world's thinking, and allow my retirement years to vanish in self-involvement and wasted time, or do I want to refocus, and ask God to show me His perfect plan for the precious time that remains?

> *"**Test me**, O LORD, and try me.*
> ***Examine** my heart and my mind..."*
> -Psalm 26:2 (NIV)

I pray that my words won't be arrogant, and echo those of Peter's before the rooster crowed. I pray that a prideful attitude won't cause me to rest on my laurels, and point to my past victories. I know the aging process will be a test of my accumulated character. I truly desire to bring honor to my heavenly Father in every stage of my life, especially now, in this last test.

Christ predicted Peter's reaction to his test. Christ has also predicted the reaction of each one of us (He knows everything!). He could even write our epitaph, our final "score," before our "roosters crow."

Do you know the truth that God knows about the motives of your heart? Do those motives truly match the words on your lips?

This final test of our character during the aging process will be very revealing. As our minds, bodies and hearts start to fail us, and we are tossed into a "sea" of challenges, our true focus will be put on display for our world to witness.

As long as we still have breath, it is never too late to start the process of change. Solomon tells us to *"Remember our Creator in the days of our youth"* (Eccl. 12:1). Spiritual youth consists of the time that comes before growth and maturing. If Solomon's words are speaking only to the physically young, then most of us might as well not even read that passage. If, on the other hand, he is encouraging us, as the spiritually young, to continue to mature and build our character, we will only be finished when we complete our earthly test and He takes us to our heavenly home.

My students know that before they take their tests I am always there to help them. I will tutor them before, or after school, at recess and/or lunchtime. If a human teacher will come alongside a student who is truly seeking help, how much more will our heavenly Teacher support and mentor us? He will bring to mind the verses we need, just as we need them. He will send people and things our way to encourage and edify us.

There is just one catch! We have to admit our need, and ask for His help.

I teach my heart out to the kids every day, looking for individual learning styles, but I don't run out to the playground at recess and force the children to accept extra assistance. The students who really care about their performance on an up-coming exam will seek me out, knock at my classroom door, and ask me for help.

Christ is always there, waiting for us to put aside our prideful, self-sufficient thinking, and to ask Him for His help. He will never slam His door on us, and in the Hands of the Holy Spirit our lives will be empowered to make an 180-degree change in motives, desires, priorities and commitment that will exhibit itself 24 hours a day, seven days a week.

O Father,

I bring my life before You. I pray "the words of my mouth and the thoughts of my heart will be pleasing to You" (Psalm 19:14). *"Test me, O LORD, and try me, examine my heart and my mind"* (Psalm 26:2), *and show me where I fail. Take every part of my body, soul and mind as a living sacrifice to You. Renew my mind.* (Romans 12:1-2) *and keep me strong to the very end* (1 Corinthians 1:7-8). *Reflect Your heart through my heart. Let me show my-world the love, goodness, kindness and patience that You have shown to me.*

May I one day stand before You and hear you say, "Well done, ... you persevered and praised My Name every day to your final day" (Psalm 119:112).

Claim Your Gold

Application Guide

Engrave your heart:
(*Memorize, or simply re-read during the day.*)

"If anyone is in Christ he is ***a new creation****; old things have past away;*
behold, all things have become new."
-2 Corinthians 5:17

"Create in me a clean heart, O God,
And renew a **steadfast** *Spirit within me."* -Psalm 51:10

"Do not be conformed to this world, but be transformed
by the ***renewing of your mind****, that you may prove what is that*
good and acceptable and perfect will of God."
-Romans 12:2

Refine the gold:

John MacArthur, Bible teacher, author, and my pastor for the past 35 years, outlines the agents of change in his book, *Twelve Ordinary Men*, which chronicles the supernatural transformation of Christ's disciples. Starting with common men, with common hopes and desires, Jesus transformed them, and renewed their minds to conform to His perfect will. The book gives hope to all its readers that true change is possible for even the weakest, most common person.

The steps of the disciples' transformation followed methods of good *teaching* and *learning*. They included:

1. Careful listening to Christ's sermons with the multitudes.

2. Jesus calling them to be personally instructed.

3. Making the commitment to follow Him.

4. Learning Godly character qualities from Christ's own life as He dealt with people. Among them were:
   a. submission.
   b. restraint.
   c. humility.
   d. love.
   e. compassion.
   f. etc.

5. Giving them ministry opportunities.

6. Patiently instructing them.

7. Graciously encouraging them.

8. Lovingly correcting them.

9. Investing His time, energy and life in their lives.

With this list of intimate fellowship between Teacher and students you would think the training was a "piece of cake." Think again! These ordinary men reflected human nature. They lacked "humility, they were self-absorbed, self-centered, self-promoting, and proud." And they were constantly arguing! On top of all this, "they lacked faith, commitment, and power." These were the men who were going to saturate the world with the gospel and help change the course of human history.

They had the training. They knew the message. They needed a 180-degree, 24/7 renewal of their minds and that's just what they received. After Christ's resurrection He sent the Holy Spirit to dwell and empower them. They immediately went from fearful deniers to bold bearers of God's truth, knowing they could *"do all things through Christ who strengthens..."*(Phil. 4:13). They were finally ready to face "all things" that lay before them. "All things," included proclaiming the gospel in public, being rejected, abused, imprisoned, and killed. The passion of the Holy Spirit saturated their lives, and temporal desires faded into the background as they invested their remaining years in sharing the gospel of eternal life through Jesus Christ, their Friend, their Teacher, their Savior and King.

They still made occasional mistakes (Gal. 2), but their hearts had been transformed to be "teachable, humble, and sensitive to the Holy Spirit's conviction and correction" 24/7.

Practical steps to a transformed life:

1. Survey your own "training" schedule.
   - -Have you asked God's forgiveness for leaving Him out of all, or part, of your life?
   - -Have you asked Him to fill your heart with the power of the Holy Spirit?
   - -Are you reading and meditating on His Word on a daily basis?
   - -Are you applying what you learn?

2. Ask God to shine the light of His truth on the motives of your heart. (It's easy to deceive ourselves into thinking we are doing everything we can do.)

3. Expect an answer, and listen to the thoughts He will faithfully bring to your mind.

4. Be sensitive to the Holy Spirit's conviction and correction. (Don't shut out your thoughts with busy, and noisy activities, and/or deny the truth when you "hear" it.)

5. Be teachable, and humble.

6. Seek the Holy Spirit's transforming power as you study and meditate on the Scriptures, daily. (Pray that you will understand what you read, and have insight into how you should apply it.)

7. Be a good steward of the gifts God has given you. (Ask Him how He wants you to use your ***talents, time, money, and resources,*** and your ***words.***)

8. Constantly thank God for His provision of empowerment (His Holy Spirit).

Nuggets of wisdom, promises and praise:
(Sing, or simply read as prayerful poetry.)

"Spirit of the Living God" by Daniel Iverson

Spirit of the Living God, fall afresh on me.
Spirit of the Living God, fall afresh on me.
Melt me, mold me, fill me, use me.
Spirit of the Living God, fall afresh on me.

Chapter 9

A Fly on the Wall

Gain Valuable Insights from the Lives of Others

insight, n.- an understanding of the motivations behind one's behavior.

Sometimes, when I see students in my classroom who have average intelligence, but "soar" above the rest of the class, and above their own abilities, I wish for the chance to be a "fly on the wall" in their homes. What are their parents doing in those homes to produce such healthy, highly motivated children? The insight would be invaluable to other parents, and to the rest of us who desire to "soar."

I also see kids with great potential who are falling further behind in their academics, and are displaying many social problems. At that point I try to get the parents involved to see how we can work together to help the child succeed. Many times we are able to come up with a workable plan and the child truly makes a 180-degree change in his or her academic life. But sometimes when I try to get the parents involved, they grudgingly come to school and give me lip-service during the conference.

"Oh yes, we'll do that!"

"O.K., I'll turn off the T.V."

"Yes, I will read to my child every night and help him learn his time tables."

How many times have I heard these promises? I can't even guess! But I know that only a very small percentage of these parents follow through with what they say. At this point in the educational process I truly would like to be that "fly " on the wall of their homes to see what is holding them back—always hoping to find an effective solution to help them to maturity.

Some people never learn to live up to their potential. They continue to blame their parents, their teachers, and their circumstances, even into their "golden" years—they never move toward maturity. If we were to look in on them, toward the end of their lives, we most likely would see them glumly riding the "merry-go-round," still wasting their God-given potential.

Perhaps you share my desire to be that "fly on the wall." Wouldn't it be insightful to "fly" into some of the Bible stories we've heard and read over the years—to see the examples up close and in person? Maybe then effective living would seem more obvious.

Undoubtedly, most of us have mentally put ourselves "on the wall" at the feet of 12-year-old Jesus as He shared His wisdom with the leaders in the temple, or later at the wedding party where He changed the water into wine, and as He fed the 5000, or as He sat and taught Mary, Martha and Lazarus in their own home. And who hasn't thought about being there as He healed the blind and the sick, called the children to "come," and when He lovingly spoke to the woman at the well? He spoke to a woman! What an example He set, showing the male-dominated culture the way to equality for all. What a privilege it would be to watch Him in action.

There are many others in the Bible who inspire "fly" fantasies! Who wouldn't love to walk with Moses, at age 80, through the parting of the Red Sea, or watch the cloud by night (God) and the pillar of fire by day (God) lead Moses and the children of Israel through the desert? What an example for all of us, of the willingness we should have to leave our *comfort zones*.

And wouldn't it be insightful to be able to ride on the shoulder of Joseph as he was betrayed by his own brothers, sold into slavery, and removed from his familiar surroundings, to be placed in the home of others. (We may also face unfamiliar surroundings some day, in the homes of our children or others.) His faithfulness to God's plan for him was incredible! What did he say to those around him as he was displaced, disgraced and shamed? Did he slander God, and blame others, or did he praise God in his everyday speech? We know the answer because we know the ending to the story. The LORD was with him (Gen. 39:2), positioning him in every trial to be in the exact spot, at the precise time that his family needed him. Through his faithfulness and perseverance, Joseph became a key figure in God's purpose for Israel. Instead of heaping anger and guilt on the heads of his brothers, he saw the bigger picture and told them. "God sent me before you to preserve life... it was not you who sent me here, but God..."(Gen. 45:5-8).

Our hope would be that as we face the changes in our bodies, our families, and our circumstances, brought on by the aging process, we will see the bigger picture, because our eyes are riveted on the Author of life. And through maturity in Christ we will model for our world what Paul taught in Romans 8:28, "And we know that all things work together for good to those who love God, to those who are the called according to His purpose."

Mary, the mother of Jesus, could see the bigger picture from the time she was a young girl. She saturated her heart and mind with the Word of God and knew the prophesies of Isaiah concerning the promised Redeemer. Who hasn't thought about being there when the angel came to tell her that the Holy Spirit would come upon her, and she would give birth to the Son of God? Who cannot feel her passion when they read her magnificent words of rejoicing and thankfulness (Luke 1:46-55)? To "hear" this humble woman giving glory to God in such an articulate way, would have been an example we could never forget. Imagine our families and friends hearing our words, in a moment of passionate thanksgiving, for being filled with His Spirit, and for being allowed to fulfill God's purpose for us in confidence and power.

We learn so much when we read God's word, and "get close" to His people, but what if we could truly see their example? How much easier it would be to understand. Good role models are so important. That is where we come in! We are the role models to our worlds, whether we display a positive character of kindness, patience, and faithfulness to God, or a negative, whining and complaining attitude—we are being watched by those we've been called to love. Our God-given duty is to reflect the goodness of Christ, and model His character.

As I began my research for facing the aging process, I thought about some of the great older people in the Bible whose lives have come to mean so much as examples of Godly character. Two of these examples are Moses, and his father-in-law, Jethro. Moses had married Zipporah, and had lived and worked with her father, Jethro, in the desert for 40 years.

God used this time to train Moses for desert living, after He had trained him for 40 years in the palace of the King of Egypt. And then, at age 80, God was ready to put His training to use in a mighty way, for He told him to "Go back to Egypt, and bring My people (Israel) out."

Out of honor and respect for Jethro, Moses went to him and requested, "Please let me go and return to my brethren who are in Egypt, and see whether they are still alive" (Ex. 4:18).

Moses had experienced Jethro's character qualities during the past 40 years. He surely knew that Jethro would give him what he needed—encouragement. It must have been a strong confirmation when this respected man said, "Go, and I wish you well." He could have made it hard for Moses to follow God, by complaining of abandonment. Jethro was probably very happy to have Moses around to tend his flocks (Ex. 3:1). He could have refused his blessing to Moses out of selfishness and stubbornness.

He could have said,

"Why in the world, would you want to do that?" or, *"You are so slow of speech, and you never know what to say! What good can you*

be for them even if they are alive?" or, he could have lied, *"God told me you were not to go! I am a priest* (not of the true God), *and you are just a shepherd."*

But God, the true God, united their hearts and thoughts, and this understanding old man sent Moses on his way.

Jethro became a very important role model. Hc, not only encouraged him to pursue God's will, he also let Moses, a younger man, lead him in praising the true God, Yahweh, later in the Exodus story (Ex. 18:7-12).

As we age, we must learn to allow God to lead us through the lives of younger people. We most likely will need the care and wisdom of those with youthful energy and insightful eyes. Instead of resisting the efforts of God's children, we must be ready to encourage them in their Christ-like behavior, and thank God enthusiastically for their willingness to serve.

Moses' respect for his father-in-law is clearly seen in Exodus 18:7-8. The Israelites, led by Moses and Aaron, had escaped Egypt and were in the desert when Jethro and Moses met again. Moses bowed down and kissed him, and then took him to his tent to tell him everything the LORD had done. He told how the LORD had handled Pharaoh and the Egyptians—for Israel's sake—about all the hardships and how the LORD had saved them.

Moses knew Jethro's mind set. He knew that he could share everything wholeheartedly and that Jethro would be delighted to hear all the good things God had done. (Are we willing to be good listeners, filled with wholehearted encouragement for God's blessings in someone else's life?)

Their hearts overflowed with praise and adoration for the power of God and His love for Israel. United in that Power they encouraged each other through their praise for His goodness (Ex. 18:11).

Knowing Jethro's heart, Moses gave much thought and consideration to his advice in the matter of his heavy workload (Ex. 18:18). Jethro did not suggest that Moses leave the people and go back home with him. Instead, he gave him a workable plan of selecting men to help him (Ex. 18:21). Jethro made it clear that in order for it to work—God must command it (Ex. 18:23). He knew this plan was from God (Ex. 18:19), but he still wanted Moses to get divine permission to implement his advice.

This is the kind of mentor, and example, we can be if we are willing to see our great potential.

We cannot leave this "fly on the wall" chapter without taking one more pass at two "silver" saints, Simeon and Anna; powerful examples of self-sacrificing faithfulness to God.

Simeon lived in Jerusalem and was a righteous and devout, hope-filled old man. He had fervently waited and watched for the promised Messiah (Luke 2:22-27). The Holy Spirit had revealed to him that he would not die until he had seen the LORD Christ (Messiah). The Spirit brought him into the temple courts just as Mary and Joseph arrived with baby Jesus—to do for Him what the custom of the Law required. In God's perfect timing, Simeon had the privilege of holding Christ in his arms and praising God for keeping His promise.

Someone else was making her way to the temple steps—the prophetess, Anna. She was an 84-year-old widow who, since her husband's death many, many years ago, had never left the temple (Luke 2:36-38).

Before the time of Jesus, women had value to society for one main purpose—child bearing. A widow, especially one without children, was seen as "nothing"—a burden, pitied by all. But not Anna! She knew the Word of God: the Books of Moses, the Psalms, and Proverbs. She spent all of her time fasting and praying—demonstrating her love and desire to be close to God. But her activities didn't end there! She obeyed God's command to "love your neighbor as yourself" (Leviticus 19:18). Through the supernatural peace that God so mightily gave her, Anna was able to reach out to her world to comfort others and to share God's blessings.

I wish I could have been there when she shared her heart as she waited for the Redeemer of the world. I can "see" her Hope being implanted into the hearts of those whose lives she touched.

With the help of the Holy Spirit and God's Word, we can learn to become someone who thanks and honors God, even in our weakest moments. We can plant "seeds" of thankfulness in the hearts of our family and friends by the example we set before them.

Anna did that! She was always looking for ways to honor her LORD. In return, God honored Anna's faithfulness. Jesus, the Savior of the world, was born a few miles away in Bethlehem, and the law required that His parents, Mary and Joseph, take Him to the temple to present Him to God.

In His perfect timing, God brought Joseph, Mary, and Jesus together on the temple steps with His two chosen witnesses, Simeon and Anna (Luke 2:25-38). Their word was trustworthy! People had viewed their lives for 60 or more years; their credibility to their world would not have been as strong if they had been younger and inexperienced. Simeon and Anna are our steadfast examples of credibility and trustworthy living.

Anna had her crowning moment; this was the crowning moment for the whole world for time and all eternity. She and Simeon were two of the most privileged people to ever live. Not only had they seen the Baby, they had assurance from God Himself that this was truly the Messiah… the Redeemer… the Savior of the world (Luke 2:26).

Before their days on earth were ended, God used them to be His witnesses to His world. Of Anna, Luke 2:38 tells us, "She gave thanks to God and spoke about the Child to all who were looking forward to the redemption of Jerusalem."

O Father,

Thank You for the insights You have taught me through the lives of Your true "silver saints." It is my prayer to be like Jethro, Simeon, and Anna. They touched the coming generations with their encouragement, their counsel and their very lives. Thank you for the many years of love You have given me. I pray that because of those years of following You, my credibility to my-world will increase during these final days. Forgive my grumbling and my forgetful spirit. Fill me with Your Spirit and turn my moaning into song.

*My desire is to one day walk into Your presence and hear You whisper in my ear, "Well done, you praised Me in the presence of my saints, and waited on My Name" (*Psalm 52:9).

Claim Your Gold

Application Guide

Engrave your heart:
(Memorize, or simply re-read during the day.)

"LORD, who may abide in Your sanctuary?...
*He whose walk is **blameless**, and who does what is **righteous**,*
and speaks the truth in his heart; and has no slander on his tongue,
who does his neighbor no wrong, and casts no slur on his fellowman..."
-Psalm 15

*"By their fruit you will know them...Every good tree bears **good fruit**,*
but a bad tree bears bad fruit."
-Matthew 7:16-18

"Who is wise? Let him understand these things.
Who is prudent? Let him know them.
*For the ways of the LORD are right; The **righteous** walk in them,*
But transgressors stumble in them."
-Hosea 14:9

Refine the gold:

Whether we like it or not, our lives produce fruit daily and that fruit is our legacy to our-world. We can only fake "good" fruit for short periods of time. Our true character is revealed, endured and reflected in our-world when life throws us a curve—when outside forces seem to be in control. Our spiritual heritage to our children, grandchildren and others, is the quality of the fruit we produce on a consistent basis, rain or shine.

The Scriptures are filled with hundreds of examples of how the harvest of good, or bad, fruit in a person's life affected a multitude of generations, many of which are still being lived out today. Adam and Eve's disobedience in the garden affects all of us continually. The ongoing problems in the Middle East can be traced to the unfaithfulness and bad decisions on the part of many Old Testament characters. Thankfully, the perfect life, death and resurrection of Jesus Christ has brought hope to the entire world.

Harvesting good fruit in our daily activities, and strengthening our example of Spirit-filled living must be a high priority as our time on earth is ticking away. Whether we have 40…20…5… or fewer years left of influence, our time is just a "vapor" compared with eternity.

It's always easier to be a good example when we have had a good example to follow. And even if we've had the privilege of many excellent role models, it never hurts to acquire one or two more.

Acquiring, evaluating and adopting character traits of Godly examples not only can help our spiritual growth, it also can be fun!

1. Start a Biblical Biographies Book Club with one or more of your friends (or read by yourself, if you prefer).

2. Read one of the biblical biographies written by Bible teacher and author, Charles R. Swindoll, (*David, Esther, Paul, etc.),* or author Francine Rivers, (*Unveiled*, giving insight into the life of Tamar, *Unashamed*, about Rahab, *Unshaken*, about Ruth, *Unspoken*, about Bathsheba, and *Unafraid* about Mary), or others.

3. Discuss each book, chapter-by-chapter, week-by-week.

4. Out of each chapter identify the Fruit of the Spirit manifested in action or words.

5. Discuss how to make practical application in your own lives during the week.

6. Thank the LORD for your "role model's" faithfulness to God.

7. Daily ask to be filled with the Holy Spirit as you seek to be a positive role model in someone's eyes.

Nuggets of wisdom, promises and praise:
(Sing, or simply read as prayerful poetry.)

"O Master, Let Me Walk with Thee" by Washington Gladden

O Master, let me walk with Thee
In lowly paths of service free;
Tell me Thy secret; help me bear
The strain of toil, the fret of care.

Help me to slow the heart to move
By some clear, winning word of love;
Teach me the wayward feet to stay,
And guide them in the homeward way.

Teach me Thy patience! Still with Thee
In closer, dearer company,
In work that keeps faith sweet and strong,
In trust that triumphs over wrong;

In hope that sends a shining ray
Far down the future's broadening way,
In peace that only Thou canst give,
With Thee, O Master, let me live. Amen.

Chapter 10

"What If…?"

Attain a God-Focused Retirement

fulfill, v.- 1. to carry out.
2. obey or follow.
purpose, n.- the reason for which something exists.

Some of the most incredible learning takes place when people get into the "What if…?" mode. "What if I had been born in a different country? What if I had learned to trust and obeyed God when I was much younger? What if a tornado, hurricane, flash flood, or earthquake shattered our lives?"

School districts, and other public agencies across the nation are now taking time to prepare employees, parents and students for pending regional disasters. Emergency procedures are set in place, practiced and evaluated During these training sessions adults, and children alike, generally slip into a "What if-ing" mode:

"What if my car gets trapped in the currents of a sudden flash flood?"

"What if I get sucked into the tornado?"

"What if my parents can't find me?"

"What if I can't locate my children, and all the buildings are destroyed?"

"What if the ground cracks open and swallows me alive?"

In a classroom filled with fearful, curious thinkers we could go on "what-ifing" forever. There's always some other creative mind working to come up with a "can you top this?" scenario.

Experienced teachers know that many of these questions stem from a true fear of not knowing what to do during a disaster. They also realize that this is a great way to distract a teacher from giving a scheduled algebra test. These students think they are so smart!

A good teacher can outsmart all such devious plots and funnel this energy and inquisitive enthusiasm into the advancement of the curriculum. I like to follow up a "What if…" moment with a creative writing assignment. "What if the teacher is knocked out during the earthquake, and you have to be in charge of your own survival?" This always gets the creative juices flowing. I've had some of the most interesting and insightful solutions manifest themselves in the students' essays.

I've used this idea once or twice a month during our literary lessons. After we read a particularly exciting selection from our anthology, we will pick it apart. We'll pull out the protagonist and discuss his or her character qualities. We then start "What-ifing." What if the hero wasn't so honest, brave, compassionate, etc? What if the "bad guy" had obeyed the rules, had not been so selfish, really did what he said he would do, etc? How would the plot of the story change? Would there be a different outcome and conclusion?

At this point we rewrite the story with some added twists and turns. It's always fun to see the results, but once we get this going the "what-ifing" never stops. I guess that is a good thing!

As we become parents, grandparents, uncles, aunts, Sunday school teachers, youth workers, etc., we can use this "what-ifing" technique with the children God places on our path. In family, private or group discussions, kids will open up, and participate in conversation with just a few "what if" questions. This is where we can learn to lovingly guide the conversation with further questions ("What do you think should be done? Why? How could we change the story? What if the good guy hadn't done the right thing?) and, most importantly, this is the time to *listen*. The insights we pick up in these moments, and the closeness we can attain, will become a bond that could endure and flourish for a lifetime.

We all have undoubtedly thought about how stories in the Bible would have ended if the characters had obeyed God's plan and had completely followed His instructions.

What if the Israelites had watched all the miracles unfold (Exodus) and then truly followed God wholeheartedly? For one thing, their journey to the Promised Land would have taken a lot less time (probably about three weeks). But their lack of obedience and trust in God caused their downfall. God punished their disobedience and constant grumbling by making them wander in the desert for 40 years (Numbers 14:33).

What if they hadn't grumbled and complained about God's provision for them?

Life for the Israelites could have been much easier and blessed—in the desert and in their new land. God clearly told them (Deut. 11) that He would bless them abundantly if they faithfully obeyed, loved, and served Him with all their heart and soul. He said it over and over. They could have had it all! But when they took to slandering God with their whining, grumbling, and lack of trust, God left them in the desert.

Of course, this was all within God's providence. Over the many years this story has been repeated, scores of people have "seen" the disobedience of the Israelites.

As we read this story, as with any Biblical story, we can accept it as just a narrative of a point in history, or we can ask, "How can I apply this to my life?" and "What is God trying to teach me that will help me please Him more?"

What if the Israelites had wholeheartedly trusted God? Would they have whined and constantly complained? God faithfully gave them manna for 40 years. People complained! After they finally crossed into the Promised Land, filled with abundant food, God stopped providing manna. People complained! What if we say we trust God, but become negative and bitter, insulting His provisions for us? On the other hand, when we thank Him in everything, we deeply touch His heart and we become the children He created us to be. Just as we desire thankful, obedient hearts from our children, God is pleased when He sees that His creations abound in all the fruit of His mighty Spirit.

What if we close down, fold up and become "shells" of weakness, contrary and negative, complaining about our lack of control over our earthly affairs? Or we could accept this part of the cycle of life, and allow the Holy Spirit to empower our attitudes, and fill our lips with praise that will glorify God, and edify those around us. That is our true purpose, and God has made it possible to attain.

The first half of my life could have been recorded and used as a warning beacon—just as the grumbling Israelites were used. But since God so mercifully changed me, and made me His new creation (2 Cor. 5:17), my hope is that I will be used as a good example to my-world. My prayer is that I will be a Moses…Joseph… Jethro… Mary… Simeon… or Anna.

Anyone (parent, grandparent, teacher, etc.) who has been involved in the learning process for any length of time knows that students (kids and adults alike) learn, so easily, to mimic bad examples and role models.

We know that Satan rules this world (Job 1:7), and he is strongly competing with God (on a daily basis) for our attention. He is so slick! He makes disobedience seem attractive, appealing, and in a number of cases—very wise. He loves to hear us grumbling and complaining against God and His Word; it is music to his ears! He is very familiar with the learning process; he knows that if he can get just one person in a group, or family, to complain and grumble—it's almost guaranteed that the rest will follow.

With constant negative input from subtle outside influences we all are being molded and changed. If we are not careful we will hear ourselves complaining and grumbling, and dishonoring the love and work that God has accomplished in our lives.

If we are to become mature, positive, Spirit-filled people we must make it a habit to—daily—ask the LORD to renew our minds. Every time we see or hear a negative, complaining comment that reflects dissatisfaction it is "recorded" in our brain and the words become part of our memory, even though we didn't verbalize them. We must go to the LORD and ask Him to shield our hearts and minds, and not allow someone else's negative words to influence our future behavior and words.

Negative "messages" from our world to our brain are so powerful, but we can take hope in the fact that Christ tells us not to be afraid—for He has "overcome the world" (John 16:33) and throughout the Psalms we are assured that God will be our shield (Psalm 3:3, Psalm 5:12, Psalm 28:7).

One of the favorite promises of all times is Philippians 4:13 which renews our hope with, *"I can do all things through Christ Who strengthens me."*

But first we have to make the decision to trust in God's strength, and not our own which is waning daily. And then we must remember to ask (Matt. 7:7) Him to renew our minds every time we hear a remark that we know would not please our Father, Savior, and Friend.

Today is the day we must start building spiritual habits that will prepare us and sustain us through our "difficult days."

O Father,

Your mercies are abundant. They allow me to learn, not just through my own mistakes, but through the mistakes, and problems of others.

What if You had left me in "my-desert" of disobedience, to become a pile of dry and useless bones? Instead You breathed Your life and Spirit into me.

My limited human tongue cannot express the gratitude that fills my heart today. I pray that one day I will have the capacity to convey adequately my love for You.

Thank You for being my shield, and for guarding my heart and mind from the tricks of Satan. My fear is that I will revert to dishonoring and slandering You with my life and with my lips. Let it never *be!*

I pray that I will one-day stand before You, and hear You say, "Well done, your heart and mouth were aligned with My truth, My love, and My kindness" (Psalm 15:1-5).

Claim Your Gold

Application Guide

Engrave your heart:
(Memorize, or simply re-read during the day.)

"Jesus said, 'You shall ***love*** *the LORD your God*
with all your heart…soul, and…mind…
You shall ***love*** *your neighbor as yourself.'*
On these two commandments hang all the Law and the Prophets."
-Matthew 22:37-40

"Therefore ***go*** *and make disciples of all nations,*
baptizing them in the Name of the Father and of the Son,
and of the Holy Spirit,
And teaching them to ***obey*** *everything I have commanded you.*
And surely I am with you always, to the very end of the age."
-Matthew 28:19-20 (NIV)

Refine the gold:

This generation of retirees and "silver saints" is probably one of the most adventuresome groups the world has ever seen. If the truth were known, the miles we've invested traversing the globe would astound the most experienced record keepers.

Does anyone see a connection between God's commandments and desires, and our ability to explore remote corners of the world, in reality, or just by a click of that little faithful "mouse"? Fulfilling the Great Commission is within our grasp!

What if instead of just getting comfortable and spending more and more time, energy and money on our own desires and comforts, we do as many older Christian have already begun? What if we rethink the world's view of retirement (ask God to renew your mind), and get into the "Moses" mode? God prepared Moses during the first 80 years of his life for humble service, and then He used him mightily in spite of his shaky, "I can't do it!" start.

We could affect generations to come if we take all the training God has given each of us, put away our negative thinking and words, and say to God, "O.K. I'm ready, now what do You want me to do?"

This doesn't mean we can't relax and have fun! Sometimes the best time to share Christ's love is when we're not focused on doing it, but it just comes out naturally. When our lives are saturated in the Living Water of the Holy Spirit, and God's Word, He will produce good fruit in us, and our world won't just hear our "sermons," they'll *see* the proof.

Grandkids, nieces, nephews, family members, friends and new friends won't really listen or seek our wisdom in times of trouble if we haven't taken the time to bond with them, and share the simple, seemingly insignificant things of their lives—a story, an ice cream cone, a trip to a new or favorite destination. Their eyes and ears are sharp and in tune. They want to know if they can trust our words—or if our words are *just words*.

What if, through negative, contrary, self-focused grumbling we slander God's provision for us, and become stumbling blocks to the faith of our-world? This kind of fear and self-centeredness set Israel back 40 years in their pursuit of the Promised Land. God's plan will prevail, but do we want our world to use their time trying to learn to trust, or growing in the trust we instill in them?

What if you:Examine your own life carefully, and count the number of negative words and attitudes you exhibit from moment–to-moment throughout each day.

1. Ask God for forgiveness, and for His power to guard your mouth mind and heart.

2. Fill your mind, daily, with positive input—**His Word**.

3. Go! Explore the world in a fun-loving, *purposeful* way.

4. Take a walk and soak in the beauty of God's creation. Thank Him!

5. Go to the market with new eyes. Survey the abundance, and choices, and thank God for His bounty.

6. Don't take life for granted. Find something to enjoy, and appreciate, even in the most ordinary circumstances.

7. Become familiar with the history curriculum that your grandkids, nieces and nephews, etc., will be studying during the coming year. Take them on a "history trip" to the area. Let them research, and be your docent for part of the trip. Play "What if…?" along the way.

8. If travel is impossible, take them to the library and help them checkout a novel (on their reading level) that will transport them through time and space, and prepare them to be ready learners. Read to or with them, and take time to snuggle and bond.

9. Write, or e-mail, missionaries that your church supports. Get involved in their family needs and desires.

10. If you are financially, and physically able, visit them, work beside them, encourage and love them.

11. Be creative! Be positive! Be willing to move out of your comfort zone.

12. Thank God in ***all*** things, and model a Christ-like attitude wherever you go.

Nuggets of wisdom, promises and praise:
(Sing, or simply read as prayerful poetry.)

"O Jesus, I Have Promised" by John E. Bode

O Jesus, I have promised to serve You to the end;
Be Thou forever near me, My Master and my Friend:
I shall not fear the battle If Thou art by my side,
Nor wander from the pathway If Thou wilt be my guide.

O let me feel Thee near me, The world is ever near;
I see the sights that dazzle, The tempting words I here:
My foes are ever near me, Around me and within;
But Jesus draw Thou nearer, And shield my soul from sin.

O Jesus You have promised To all who follow Thee,
That where Thou art in glory, There shall Thy servant be;
And, Jesus, I have promised To serve Thee to the end;
O give me grace to follow, My Master and my Friend.

Chapter 11

"Just Joking!"

Guard Your Mouth; Keep Your Sense of Humor

joking, v.- to say something in fun or teasing rather than in earnest.

It is always fun to see how a story would end if the main character did everything with integrity and selfless caring, but sometimes it is more instructive to imagine the ending of a story on the premise of a negative "What if."

Anna and Simeon's lives in their community intrigue me more and more. Working through how they handled their blessing of old age is the purpose of all my research.

Being used by God in a powerful way, as these two "silver" saints were used, would bring our lives to a triumphal culmination. Their words were not hollow, "lip-service" tokens to God. Their lives exuded their overwhelming faith and love for Him. When they said they had seen the Savior, people believed them. They each had a reputation for speaking the truth. People that heard their testimony didn't laugh and disregard their words, or think they were just joking, as Lot's son's-in-law did when Lot tried to save his family from God's wrath at Sodom (Gen. 19:14).

Think about Lot for a minute. He was righteous, by faith, before God, and yet he was spiritually weak. He hated the sins of Sodom, but his testimony was compromised because he had let the negative culture influence his thinking and behavior. He thought he was doing right when he tried to protect visiting strangers from a lustful mob. He actually offered his own daughters to the crowd in order to protect his guests (Gen. 19).

O Lot! What were you thinking?

What if Lot had led a strong, God-fearing, credible (even fun-filled) life during his years in Sodom? The course of history could have been drastically changed! When he spoke to his sons-in-law to warn them, they wouldn't have laughed at his warning (Gen. 19:14), or thought it was just some legalistic ploy to get them to follow. If they had witnessed the power and truth of God in Lot's life throughout the years they would have undoubtedly listened—maybe even helped Lot in the moving process. They could have been another "Noah's family." They could have made God smile.

What if Simeon and Anna were just legalistic Jews of their day? What if in place of seeking God's Face through the Scriptures, prayer, and sharing that experience with others, they resorted to legalistic rules? They might have become very prideful in their efforts. Instead of reaching out with the joys of following God, they could have demanded honor to be focused on themselves (Luke 2:38).

The majority of the Pharisees of the day did just that. They sought the favor and honor of men instead of seeking God's will. They piled the rules and demands higher and higher on the backs of the people they were called to serve (Matthew 23:4-7). God had told them clearly in His Word to:

> *"See that you do all I command you;*
> *do not add to it or take away from it."*
> -Deuteronomy 12:32 (NIV)

So what happened? Did they forget to continue to read God's Word? Did their memories become fuzzy and engulfed in tradition?

Did they think they were doing God a favor by adding more and more requirements to His law? Did they fall into the old cliché…"If a little medicine is *good*, more must be *better*!"

Christ's harshest words while He was here on earth were directed at the self-righteous Pharisees, Scribes, and moneychangers (Matt. 23:27). They were the ones responsible for adding rules and overcharging the poor in the temple courtyard by inflating the price that the weary travelers had to pay for an appropriate sacrifice. They were the guardians of their faith—but they were making it harder, rather than easier, for people to honor God.

We've all heard the old saying, "Absolute power corrupts, absolutely!" and unfortunately, we've all seen it played out on the front pages of our newspapers and the evening news. Through unbelieving eyes we have watched the downfall of truly sincere politicians, police officers, ministers and the CEOs of large corporations, etc., who seemingly began their careers with the desire to lead with integrity. They once knew what was fair and right, and in many situations they allowed the truth to prevail, and their decisions were "applauded," their power increased.

And then one day the stress of problems, temptations, and/or their greedy need for more power, helped to compromise their integrity and fairness. They become politically and selfishly motivated; not for the good of the people they were called to lead, but for self-advancement and recognition. Integrity, and thoughts of fairness and equity flew out the window as devious manipulations stomped on the hearts of trusting followers. Helplessly, the followers try to pick up the pieces of their lives and restore their faith in the system that they once trusted.

One of Christ's most urgent goals, as He walked the dusty roads of Israel, was to restore the integrity of the temple and deal justly with the "thieves" who were in charge. Christ's passion and protection for the purity of the temple was dramatically displayed as He angrily knocked over the tables and cleared-out the moneychangers (Matt. 21:12). This is a vivid picture for us, for if we truly have the Holy Spirit living within our hearts we can be confident in the fact that Christ will do the same for us. He will fiercely protect and cleanse our "temple" if we allow His good Name to be crowded out (Prov. 11:23). His justice is sure and balanced! God ***is*** love, as we hear repeated again and again in our culture, but "prophets" of this age forget to add that He is also just (Psalm 37:28). Psalm 33:5 reminds us of His love for *justice* and *righteousness.*

Except for the grace and purpose of God, Anna and Simeon could have fallen in step with the self-serving, hypocritical leaders of their day. What if they had forsaken righteousness and had become part of that temple culture? Would God have blessed them with the privilege of seeing Christ if they had had blinders tightly covering their eyes, and their minds and hearts closed to truth? Would people have believed their testimony of being with the long awaited Messiah and looking into the Face of God?

What if Anna had followed the course of most widows of her time and just stopped "living." She could have easily gone to her cave of isolation and self-pity, becoming a burden and a "victim." She could have become an imposing, bitter old woman seeking the reinforcing pity of all who dared to come near. She might have echoed the Israelites of the desert and slandered God by grumbling and complaining about her fate.

We've all been there! Whether through the death of a loved one, a crippling accident or disease, financial setbacks, or other desperate times, we've all had trouble. The Bible tells us that this life will be filled with trouble (John 16:33). How we handle—or don't handle—our trouble is exactly the training we need to prepare us for the *trouble* of old age.

The "widows" group in our church is a beautiful example of maturity and love. It began with the sudden death of one of the elders. Church members surrounded his grieving wife 24/7 for the first several months. She was never alone, as the ladies of the congregation set up a schedule for dinners and care.

This present-day "Anna" could have become dependent on all the attention, and maintained a "victim" role, but she was the first one at the side of the next widow, and the next. Over the years this group has sheltered and encouraged many wounded hearts.

These women have lived quiet lives before the eyes of the church. They model for us the "Anna" attitude of Spirit-filled lives that reflect and honor Gods unmatchable grace. Those with little, or no faith in the plan and purpose of God, have been heard to mock, and ridicule His wisdom and love, but not these women! Sadness penetrates the "spouse-shaped" vacuum left in their hearts, and yet, they know that their only hope is in the LORD, and His comforting, compassionate Hand.

Life is a cycle. We all know that for 100% of us, life will end in death, and yet, when it happens we act surprised. Survival mode is human nature, built into us by God Himself, for the purpose of persevering through multitudes of trials. Our character will either honor or dishonor God in the process.

In the long run God will not be mocked or dishonored (Gal. 6:7)! He will surely display His justice in every situation and His timing is perfect! The Pharisees and the moneychangers had been robbing the poor in their temple enterprises for many, many years. God's Word said they were to take care of the widows, orphans, and the poor (Deut. 14:29), and yet they blatantly took advantage of those they were charged to protect. God was patient. He waited for the perfect moment to dispense His justice. All the "pieces" and "players" had to be in position in order to highlight this occasion—it would teach everyone who has ever heard, or read, this story a "secondhand" lesson. Oh, that we might take it to heart and learn the easy way—through someone else's failures!

Pray that we won't become self-imposed "victims" in the years to come. Pray that ***we*** will not be swallowed by the "wolf" of Little Red's nightmare.

Suppose Red's "wolf" had devoured Anna. She might have spent her days simply "people watching" on the steps of the temple, waiting and watching for someone else to whom she could complain. She might have reached out a frail old hand and clutched at anyone who strayed too close. Upon capturing their attention she might have jealously detained them from their true mission at the temple—worshipping God. She could have complained about everything: "The food is so bland here… The bed is too hard…I'm always freezing in my drafty stone chamber."

She could have been so wrapped up in her self-centered thoughts, that the honor she should have reflected to God was, instead, being absorbed by her self-pity.

We've all known people like "wolf-eaten" Anna; they've existed in every family since time began. They thrive on complaining and negative statements. They dishonor God's provisions for them, and chase people away with their critical, sharp remarks. Their very own lips destroy what they desire most in life—attention and companionship.

Many of us have witnessed this type of behavior over and over again! And even though our lips say, "Remind me never to get like that," our minds are recording the negative input, day after day. Unless we give more than just "lip-service" to our fears of conforming to this self-serving standard, we also might hear the same poisonous words tumbling out of our own mouths. That evil "wolf" might devour us, and the Little Reds of our world will unfortunately have our negative grumbling etched on their brains.

Generation after generation, the "wolf" is faithfully waiting at the door (Gen. 4:7). But we have another door, and all we have to do is "see" the danger and knock, and Christ will let us in (Matt. 7:7). He will up hold us in His mighty Hand (Psalm 63:8), and teach us what pleases Him.

Oh, that we might please Him!

O Father,

You have given me so many good examples through Your Word, and through those around me. I pray that their loving, kind, and gentle ways will be etched deeply into my mind and heart. When my memory for names, dates, and facts slips away, I pray that Your love and compassion will be indelible. Whether I remember the names of the people You send my way, or not, let me always remember how to earnestly reflect Your goodness.

I have heard many derogatory and slanderous words in my lifetime; unfortunately, they have been indelibly recorded in my mind. I pray that You will "renew my mind," and help me escape the negative patterns of this world (Romans 12:1-2).

May I one day stand before You and hear You say, "Well done... you constantly sought to find My will—you renewed your mind daily with My good and perfect will." (Roman 12:2)

Claim Your Gold

Application Guide

Engrave your heart:
(Memorize, or simply re-read during the day.)

"It is good and fitting for one to eat and drink,
and to ***enjoy*** *the good of all his labor...*
all the days of his life which God gives him... "-Ecclesiastes 5:18
"Be wise in the way you act... make the most of every opportunity.
Let your conversation be always ***full of grace****, seasoned with salt,*
so that you may know how to answer everyone."
-Colossians 4:5-6 (NIV)

Refine the gold:

Enjoyment of life is one of the goals of most retirees. Enjoyment is an active endeavor; it is **not** synonymous with laziness or foolishness. We must continue to walk in wisdom and carefully plan and use the time that remains. Our conversations must constantly reflect God's truth. We never know when there may be an "outsider" (someone who doesn't know of God's goodness), a weak believer, or a child within earshot of our words.

Lot was considered righteous before God—righteous, but weak. God carefully removed him from the destruction of Sodom, and told him to take his family. Unfortunately, part of his family (his sons-in-law) thought he was just joking. This leads us to believe that he did a lot of joking, and his words were not always credible.

Have you ever been around people like that? (Or maybe you've caught yourself turning everything into a joke.) They say things with a straight face, and once they see they've "got you," they laugh, "*Just joking*!" After they "get you" several times you learn the art of "not buying in."

Does that mean we can't joke? Of course not! Every good speech, presentation or sermon usually includes at least one lighthearted antidote, even from the most serious, God-fearing speakers. We have been gifted with the capacity to laugh and enjoy life. That's where wisdom and balance come in. We must always evaluate our words to see if they contradict God's truth.

Don't speak before you think! Evaluate your joke and pretend your audience is Christ Himself. *"Inasmuch as you did* (said) *it to one of the least of these My brethren, you did* (said) *it to Me"* (Matt. 25:40). Will He be please that you gladdened the hearts of His "children"? Or will He cringe with your insensitivity to His truth?

When I hear people joking, "We better say grace before we eat or we might be poisoned," or other silly foolishness, I cringe. What are we teaching those around us? We don't know their true spiritual condition.

Prepare before you try to bring laughter to your world.

1. Fill your mind with God's truth, daily.

2. Ask the LORD to guard your mouth, and quicken your mind.

3. Ask for forgiveness when you "blow it"; we all do!

4. Ask the Father to shield the minds of your listeners when you do "blow it." Apologize to them for your insensitivity. (Don't make apologies by blame-shifting. Take responsibility for your inappropriate words. Don't repeat them to a different audience.)

5. Collect God-honoring jokes. (So many are circulating on the Internet.)

6. Refine several funny family stories, and practice the art of ***good*** storytelling.

7. Thank God for the ability to enjoy life.

Nuggets of wisdom, promises and praise:
(Sing, or simply read as prayerful poetry.)

"Joyful, Joyful, We Adore Thee" by Henry van Dyke

Joyful, joyful, we adore Thee, God of glory, Lord of love;
Hearts unfold like flowers before Thee, Opening to the sun above.
Melt the clouds of sin and sadness, Drive the dark of doubt away;
Giver of immortal gladness, Fill us with the light of day.

All Thy works with joy surround Thee, Earth and heaven reflect Thy rays,
Stars and angels sing around Thee, Center of unbroken praise.
Field and forest, vale and mountain, Flowery meadow, flashing sea,
Chanting bird and flowing fountain, Call us to rejoice in Thee.

Thou art giving and forgiving, Ever blessing, ever blessed,
Well-spring of the joy of living, Ocean depth of happy rest!
Thou our Father Christ, our Brother—All who live in love are Thine;
Teach us how to love each other, Lift us to the joy divine.

Mortals, join the happy chorus Which the morning stars began;
Father love is reigning o'er us, Brother love binds man to man.
Ever singing, march we onward, Victors in the midst of strife,
Joyful music leads us sunward In the triumph song of life.

Chapter 12

"Wolf-Eaten" or Spirit-Filled

Outgrow Grumbling and Complaining

self-serving, adj.- preoccupied with one's own selfish interests and often disregarding the truth and well-being of others.
grumbling, v.- an expression of discontent; complaint.

Simeon and Anna were passionately committed to the promises of God. They didn't have the benefit of the gospel's account of Christ's sacrificial death and resurrection. Their Scriptures were limited to a few Old Testament books—they didn't even know there would be a New Testament. But they had God's promises of Israel's coming Redeemer.

In her role as prophetess (Luke 2:36), Anna was in the temple, day and night—enlightening others in the depths of the Word of God. The passion could be seen in her eyes as she recounted God's faithfulness to Israel and His personal goodness to her. Listeners would watch her eyes fill with joyous tears as she reflected God's love with a thankful heart. "Why has He chosen me to proclaim His Word?" she might have puzzled. "I am no one! A lowly widow." Quickly her questions would turn to praise and adoration, and it was all she could do to wait for the next person she could tell.

She knew God's requirements for worship. She knew that when the Savior was born, His parents must bring Him to only one place—the temple—to dedicate Him to the LORD. She was going to be there! She would wait and watch for His coming as long as God allowed her to live.

She was there that day—along with Simeon. Their hopes and joys were fulfilled! The Light of the World sparkled, and was reflected in her old, dim eyes. Her overflowing heart energized her wobbly, frail ancient body.

"...she gave thanks to the LORD and spoke of Him
to all those who looked for redemption in Jerusalem."
-Luke 2:38

What a picture that must have been, and yet, it could have been so different, if Anna hadn't had her eyes focused, and waiting. Imagine, for a moment, how it might have ended for a "wolf-eaten," self-serving, grumbling Anna.

From their early childhood, Joseph and Mary had been carefully trained to respect their elders, and to care for the widows and the fatherless. Taking this duty seriously, they step forward to greet this old woman as they approach the steps of the temple with Jesus. They listen with patience and respect to her "victim" voice as she grumbles and complains about everything under the sun. They try to get her to see the Glory of God they're cradling in their arms, but all Anna can see with her dim, unfocused eyes are the swaddling clothes in which the Son is wrapped.

"Too tight!" she croaks. "You've wrapped it too tight!

"Why, in my day we were taught as young girls the right way to swaddle a baby. What's the matter with you?"

We can almost see Joseph catch Mary's eye with encouragement, and try to tactfully, and respectfully, continue their pilgrimage. They both silently agree to use the other steps as they leave—for why should this most joyous day be brought low with such negative grumbling, and self-serving, disparaging remarks?

Why would "Anna-of-the-wolf" settle for such a sad and lonely life (unfortunately, others had probably tried to avoid her)? The blessings of her compassionate, loving Father, were waiting right at the edge of her self-centered world.

In truth we all know why she grumbled and complained. We've been there! We all want people to love and care about us. It's human nature!

Being a "victim" will attract people who truly have a heart to honor, respect and help those in need. But as these "good Samaritans" try to minister to someone who would rather wallow in self-pity than to share in the promises of God, they silently slip away, and move on to others in need of uplifting encouragement.

As a true sufferer of an illness or injustice, you've probably felt the love and care of those around you, people who have stepped forward to be God's comfort and strength in your time of greatest need. When the crisis has passed, it is quite tempting to remain in the "victim" role, and not move toward maturity. But God has called us to be victors—not whining, complaining "victims." He has pursued us to fill us with love, joy and all the fruit of His Holy Spirit, for the purpose of reaching out to *others* in true need.

I remember always having very strong feelings about the things of God. Was God pursuing me?

As a young child my parents would, occasionally, take our family to a small neighborhood church and then send me off to a Sunday school class for kids my age. The elderly teacher seemed kind enough, but when she started talking about Judas' betrayal of Christ she betrayed her own mission.

She asked the class if we could guess how many pieces of silver Judas received for information about Jesus. I didn't know many Bible stories, but I knew Christ was the Savior of the world—God in human form. I was extremely, and painfully shy, but something inside of me blurted out with great conviction, "It must have been a million!"

At that point, everyone in the room roared with laughter.

I didn't think I had said anything that funny, so I guessed my answer was way off base. I could feel the heat fill my face, and I hoped the kind teacher would quickly put an end to the laughter. When it didn't stop, I glanced out of the corner of my eye at Mrs "Lip-Service." She was laughing louder than the rest! As she saw me peek at her she let out her last little chuckle, rolled her eyes, and patted me on the head. "That's O.K., Sweetie," she chortled. "We know you don't come here very often. Maybe if you did, you would know the correct answer is '30.'"

Was this her way of feeling superior and important? Did she have to prove her "wisdom" by putting someone else (a very young child) to shame, or was she simply insensitive–enjoying the laugh of the moment? How would Jesus have answered me? (Mark 9:36-37).

I pleaded with my parents never to make me go back, but I didn't tell them why. I didn't want them to know I had disgraced them with my stupidity. On subsequent trips to church they would let me sit through the over-my-head sermons of "big church" with them.

I could have been nurtured and started on my path to God if my teacher had seen her role as reflecting His love.

Would God have been pleased with her, and honored her, for patiently and kindly correcting me? He tells us that whatever we do unto the least, we do unto Him (Matt. 25:45). Loving God is our purpose whether we honor and exalt Him directly, or through the lives of those He puts on our path.

God continued to pursue me!

During my freshman year in high school my uncle sought out my dad to come work for him as manager of a small lumber company out in the California High Desert. My sister and I hated the change with a passion, because it meant we had to leave our friends and city life. On the other hand, our little brother loved the lizards and snakes, and couldn't understand why his older siblings were so upset. We had moved from a nice, medium-sized southern California town to a postage stamp-sized desert community of less than 3,000 people. There was no T.V.! There was barely any radio reception. Thank goodness we did have electricity and indoor plumbing.

As I look back now, I know that this was all in God's providence and plan for me. Our only social outlet, besides school, was the small church on the corner (about 35 people on a good Sunday). All the kids our age seemed to gravitate to that corner on Saturday nights. Someone had had some forethought about how to bring the youth into the church. They had built a large, still unfinished, cement roller skating rink. The walls had risen just high enough to be used as benches and then the money ran out. Every Saturday afternoon we would spend an hour or two sweeping a week's supply of wind-blown desert sand off the slab. We'd throw together some snacks and sodas—and "Voila!"...our fun began!

Many warm summer desert nights we spent skating under God's magnificent canopy of stars. If the Sunday preaching and the annual evangelist hadn't convinced me of God's existence, His glorious nightly show cinched the deal. I wanted to please Him! I wanted to do everything I could for Him. I either missed the lesson on submission to His will for my life there, or they never taught it.

My sister and I and some of our friends went full-speed ahead—searching for things to do at that tiny refuge in the desert. We sang in the choir, we lead the youth group, and we established and printed a small newspaper and weekly bulletin. When I say "printed"—I mean mimeographed. Our fingers were covered with jet-black ink every Saturday. We were a strong, take-charge kind of group!

Our pastor loved having us around because we got so much done, and... he *truly* loved us! He and his wife were involved in every project we decided to pursue. Their lives were saturated with God's love, kindness, gentleness, and joy. Their Spirit-filled lives overflowed daily into our group activities and to our individual needs. I wanted what they had, and I tried to attain it in my own power. I was in church every time the doors opened. Many times the group of us would sneak in the back door to work on some new, creative idea we had hatched.

Tears of excitement and sorrow streamed down our faces as we walked the aisle of our high school graduation ceremony. Some of us were off to college, others to full-time jobs or marriage. We knew our precious days of collegiality were ending. We knew that no matter how hard we worked at maintaining our bonded hearts, we would never again be the same.

Now and then I think back on those wonderful, God-given four years of my life. I compare them with the 40 years Moses spent in the desert. Just as Moses met God in the desert (Exodus 4)—so did I. He moved me back to the city for my college years, trained me, and then started me on my journey. But, because I still didn't "get" the submission part of the path He had planned for me, I spent many, very hard, unproductive years wandering in my self-created "desert." I worked so hard—yet my life was falling apart. The love and acceptance I sought was elusive. Even my grumbling cries of "victim" didn't bring the peace, joy and love promised in God's word.

There had to be a better way!

It took many years of endless trials and upheaval before I finally came to the end of myself, and my own efforts, and truly started seeking God's will for my life. At that point, God restored me to His perfect and exciting path that He had set out for me before the foundation of the earth (Eph. 1:3-4).

The moment I submitted my whole heart to Him, He moved my self-built "house" from the foundation I had started building on the sand, to His chosen, solid foundation of the *Rock* of obedience (Matt. 7:24-27). He even gave me housewarming gifts... *overwhelming peace, incredible joy* and a *love* I'd been seeking all my life!

O Father,

Thank You for Your loving patience with me. Forgive me for wasting so many precious years in a self-serving pursuit of happiness. Forgive me for thinking that if I submitted my life to Your plan, I would be bored and restricted, bound by rules, and forbidden to enjoy the time I have on earth.

Thank You for the upheaval and lack of peace You allowed me to experience. It finally brought me to the end of my prideful, self-righteousness generated by doing many "wonderful" and "good" things. Thank You for not blessing my efforts and for shattering my confidence. Thank You for eroding the "sand" of my foundation, and causing my *house to fall.*

You reached down and pulled me out of the sandy, "slimy pit" (Psalm 40:2 -NIV*) of my own making, and set my house on the foundation of obedience to You. You are so compassionate and patient! Let me reflect that character and nature to my-world.*

Let me one day stand before You and hear You say, "Well done, you selflessly reached out in love just as I commanded." (Matthew 22:37-40)

Claim Your Gold

Application Guide

Engrave your heart:
(Memorize, or simply re-read during the day.)

"Turn my ***heart*** *toward Your statutes and* not *toward selfish gain."*
-Psalm 119:36 (NIV)

"I have considered my ways and have turned my ***steps*** *to Your statutes."*
-Psalm 119:59 (NIV)

"May those who fear You rejoice when they see me,
for I have put my ***hope*** *in Your Word."*
-Psalm 119:74 (NIV)

Refine the gold:

Judas betrayed Christ. For three years, while he was walking closely with Jesus, the world thought he was truly one of Christ's men. Even the other eleven apostles trusted him enough to make him their treasurer. Christ called him *"friend."*

Judas may have even thought he was on the right track and he would be part of the leadership group when Christ set up His kingdom on earth. When he realized that Christ's teachings pointed to a spiritual kingdom and not an earthly, "conquer-the-Romans" kingdom, he became disillusioned. He had hoped for some kind of material reward for all the time he had invested in following this Man.

He never loved this Man, Christ, or the purpose for which He came. Judas was wrapped up in himself and what he could get out of this association.

His world was surprised! They couldn't believe that one of their own would betray their Friend. The Apostle John even asked, *"Lord, who is it?"* (John 13:25) The eleven were perplexed; they didn't seem to have a clue! Not until Judas removed his "sheep's clothing" and revealed the "wolf" inside.

There are many betrayers today who associate themselves with God's Name. These people know how to "play the game" and manipulate people and situations for their own self-interest. They hope there will be some kind of material, health or psychological reward for their invested efforts and time. They never truly love the LORD, their God and Savior, or seek to please Him through obedience and submission to His Word.

These are the people who give the Good News a bad name. By their lives, and through their grumbling, self-righteous, prideful tongues they profane God's beauty, His promises, and His Holy Name.

At this point I'm sure we are all thinking of someone we know that fits the description. Unfortunately, there are many among us! People who either haven't taken the "Bridge" of Christ to God, or those who have, but are still trying to do things in a way that would glorify themselves, and not God.

Are they among us, or are they us?

Jesus gives us a very humorous image as He warns us against hypocrisy and a condemning spirit (not against true discernment), rising from self-righteousness. In Luke 6:41 He asks, *"Why do you look at the speck in your brother's eye, but do not perceive the PLANK in your own eye?"*

1. Ask God to take your blinders from your eyes.

2. Ask the LORD to help you walk in truth as you examine your own words, and motives.

3. Honestly "record" (mentally or in writing, or if you're really brave, on tape) all of your statements for several days.

4. Listen to yourself. What are others really hearing? What is God hearing? Are you, indirectly, berating His provisions through grumbling? Are you causing others to grumble?

5. Do people avoid you due to your, negative, disparaging and/or manipulative words? (Ask for God's insight.)

6. For at least one week (or, for the rest of your life), be tuned-in, and sensitive to the body language and words of those with whom you speak.

7. Don't resort to blame shifting. Take responsibility for your part in the outcome of every conversation. (The goal is to edify the other person, and leave them with a thankful heart.)

8. Ask for forgiveness, and help from the Holy Spirit,…

9. OR (hopefully), after careful inspection, your obedience to His Word will be confirmed and you can thank Him for His indwelling Holy Spirit that produces only good fruit.

10. Saturate your mind with a review of the fruit of the Spirit—

"love, joy, peace, kindness, goodness, gentleness,
patience, self-control, faithfulness" (Galatians 5:22-23)

"Not everyone who says to Me, 'Lord, Lord,'
will enter the kingdom of heaven,
but only he who does the will of My Father who is in heaven."
-Matthew 7:21 (NIV)

Nuggets of wisdom, promises and praise:
(Sing, or simply read as prayerful poetry.)

"The Solid Rock" by Edward Mote

My hope is built on nothing less
Than Jesus' blood and righteousness;
I dare not trust the sweetest frame,
But wholly lean on Jesus' Name.
Refrain:
On Christ, the solid Rock, I stand—All other ground is sinking sand,
All other ground is sinking sand.

When darkness veils His lovely face,
I rest on His unchanging grace;
In every high and stormy gale
My anchor holds within the veil.

Refrain:
On Christ, the solid Rock, I stand—All other ground is sinking sand,
All other ground is sinking sand.

His oath, His covenant, His blood
Supports me in the whelming flood,
When all around my soul gives way,
He then is all my hope and stay.
Refrain:
On Christ, the solid Rock, I stand—All other ground is sinking sand,
All other ground is sinking sand.

When He shall come with trumpet sound,
O may I then in Him be found
Dressed in His righteousness alone,
Faultless to stand before the throne.
Refrain:
On Christ, the solid Rock, I stand—All other ground is sinking sand,
All other ground is sinking sand.

Chapter 13

Don't Just "Get Through It!"

Make Every Interaction an Opportunity

opportunities, n.- a situation favorable for attainment of a goal.
now, adv.- without further delay; immediately.
prepare, v.- to put things or oneself in readiness;
get ready beforehand.

What if God-given faith had not drawn us to ask God to show us His way for our lives, and give us His wisdom? (James 1:5).

What if I had continued on my showy, self-centered path? My future (on that sandy foundation) would have been what I have seen in the bitter, "Why me?" lives of self-righteous "saints." The result of bitterness is displayed in the lives of the chosen nation (Israel) who God left, grumbling and complaining, on the sands of the desert. And in the stories of the Pharisees, who put themselves above the very throne of God in their efforts to create and control their own showy, religious order.

Through these examples, and the negative, contrary, complaining lips of modern day examples, God has graciously shown us a gigantic yellow warning sign. For… *"Except by the grace of God, there go I."*

If those around us see our lack of faith and trust in God's provisions, our disparaging words will be permanently etched in their brains, and eventually be re-run for their world on the "screens" of their lives.

Solomon says **"now"** is the time we must **prepare**. Now is the time to **examine** our lives, and **remember** our God-given path and purpose for the days we've yet to see.

"If you have the faith, even as small as a mustard seed... nothing will be impossible for you" (Matt. 17:20), even glorifying God through an old and decaying body.

"But... but!" you say, *"Why dwell on this 'aging' thing? Why not just take it as it comes?"*

God says in Luke 12:26, not to worry about anything.

Of course we are not supposed to worry! And there are people who pride themselves in never planning, because they equate planning with worrying. They charge on through their lives, taking each moment as it comes—planning and preparing for nothing. They see each day as just something they have to "get through." They know they have to just "get through" five… four… three more days before the weekend… the "big game"… the holiday, etc. They wish their lives away! As they wait for that special event down the line, they forget to prepare for the very next person God puts on their path, or the next challenge, or sunset, or trial, or blessing. It's all a blur! *"Just get through it!"*

Why would Solomon, the wisest man to live (1 Kings 4:29-31), tell us to think of these things "now?" (Eccl. 12:1). Isn't God with us, working out His purpose? Why do we have to remember ***now*** to prepare? Won't life just happen?

Why did God tell Joshua, in Joshua 8:1-3, to gather his 30,000 best fighting men, and tell them to "listen carefully" to his plan for taking the city of Ai? Why did he need a plan? Wasn't God with him? Why couldn't he just kick back, relax, and let it unfold, and… *"Just get through it?"*

Before Joshua and the Israelites had even crossed the Jordan River to put themselves in position for the battles of Jericho and Ai, God had specifically told them to, "Get ready!" (Joshua 1:2). But God had already told them He would go with them, and if they obeyed His Word, He would never leave them, or forsake them (Deut. 31:6). He had also said He would give them the whole land (Deut. 34:4, Joshua 1:3), so why did they have to "get ready"?

If they wanted the blessings and protection of God, they knew from past mistakes that they had to obey His every word. God said to "get ready," and so they got ready! But what did that mean? What did they have to do? Did they just have to get ready to "get through it," or was there more?

God was ready to help them not only take possession of the land He had promised them, but also to build their trust and faith in Him.

God could have quickly wiped the land clean, and telepathically put all the people in place. It would have been easy! It could have been over and accomplished in the twinkling of an eye! But the purpose of God was not just the land. He wanted their hearts, their love, and their devotion. He was setting the backdrop, involving their will to plan and obey, and moving them to possess a larger capacity for trusting Him.

Humanly speaking, it is impossible to learn to trust someone, or something, if we never see the need for trust. We can give "lip-service" to our ability to trust, but until it is proven, "trust" is just a word.

Joshua had spent 40 years intently watching the Hand of God at work in the life of Moses. He learned that when there was obedience in the camp, God blessed, and he knew the result of rebellious behavior was always the cause of fear. Joshua, in his God-given wisdom (Deuteronomy 34:9), took all of God's Word to heart (Deuteronomy 32:46). He knew if God said, *"Get ready"... "Be strong"... "Be very courageous"... "Meditate on My words, day and night"... "Carefully obey"* (Joshua 1:1-9 -NIV), he would be abundantly blessed if he obeyed.

As a teacher, I know that the most learning occurs when the students are prepared to learn. If their focus and attention are somewhere else, and all they want to do is "get through it," I can stand on my head and tap dance, and the kids will still be "kids." However, if I take the time to set the scene, motivate ("salt") them, show thcm a need, and help them prepare to learn, I can take 100 "kids" and turn them into thirsty students who want to truly learn what I have to teach.

That is my challenge every year as I get a fresh "mission" field (teaching the "natives" to read). Young minds walk into my room at varying times during the day. They come in all stages of preparedness. Some are already students—prepared and wanting to learn. Others slink in with a glazed "just-try-to-teach-me" look in their eyes—eyes which are glued to the hands of the clock, just waiting to "get through it."

Before I even have a chance to turn them into life-long learners, I have to prepare them to see a need for what I have to offer. I also have to build their confidence in me so they will trust that what I am saying is true and meaningful to their lives.

The pay-off for a teacher is not when they memorize their times tables, learn the Preamble, or pass the state mandated tests with proficiency (not that this hurts, mind you!), but the true pay-off is when I see them become thirsty, eager learners! Sometimes it takes a month or two, sometimes half a year, but eventually, if I shed enough "light" on the subject, and sprinkle enough "salt" all around, I get to see my love of learning reflected in their eyes. For me, that's what it's all about!

By studying the unmatchable teaching skills and methods that Christ used in His earthly "classroom," we are able to see how He motivated His students to use the "platform" of each and every problem they faced, to mature their walk with Him, and advance the kingdom of God. Teaching them to "just get through your last days on earth" was *never* an option!

He had only a few short years to prepare His men for what lay ahead. They had skills and passion, but He had to teach them to reach out in love. He skillfully used common, visual aids in almost every situation. He had to show them they had a need for all the wisdom He was trying to share with them. When someone didn't "get it" He would approach the subject again, and again, with different stories and illustrations. He kept reminding them that they had to focus with their eyes and ears (Matt. 13:16-17). He was their role model as He lovingly washed their feet (John 13:5-7) and cooked their breakfast (John 21:9-13). He was there with, and for them in every situation. He made it a point to connect with them on their level, using their terminology to engage them in His plan. He spent three intense years of preparation with them so they would be ready to face their future. He filled them with knowledge, love and trust.

Using their newly acquired skills they were then able point others toward Christ, the "Bridge" to God. They were confident in their hearts that they had been called, trained and nurtured to spread their urgent message to the world. Their faith in Christ developed step-by-step. God prepared them and trusted them to follow through! Now, God is trusting us to prepare and follow through!

Good preparation and constant focus help us persevere even in times of distress.

When Christ their teacher, role model and authority was suddenly whisked away that dreadful night, they fearfully denied it all! They panicked, ran, and lied about their involvement as Christ's students (Matthew 26:56, 74). Their learning to trust wasn't quite cemented in their hearts. There was one last step to their training—His promised resurrection! When Christ appeared to them three days after His death, they knew they could trust Him and His careful instructions. They obeyed Him, even as He ascended to heaven, and left them alone. He told them to wait in the city (Acts 1:4), and now they were eager to wait. The pieces were all coming together. They were excited to see the next part of the puzzle. As soon as they were prepared, focused and ready, God came into them in the power of His Holy Spirit. Now they were ready to face their world, occupied by self-righteous doubters. They were even ready to go to their own "cross" if they had to, as they spread the "light" and sprinkled the "salt." No longer were they thinking of just "getting through it." Now they were equipped and prepared to passionately glorify their Friend… their Savior… their God.

These common but well prepared men are our God-given role models. They stand before us, pointing the way from passive surrender and mediocrity, to victorious excellence, and Godliness.

O Father,

When I think of my life and how You have led me, step-by-step to this very day, I am overwhelmed with gratitude! So many pieces of the puzzle – good and bad – have brought me to this moment. You have used each piece to deepen me, and show me Your power. Truly, "all things work together for good for those who love You" (Romans 8:28).

Fill me with Your light, and make the words of my mouth "salty" that my-world will be thirsting for Your living water (Matthew 5:13-16, John 4:14).

Focus my eyes to "see," and my ears to "hear" the plans You have for me as I face these coming years. Thank you for them.

Show me now, how to properly prepare so that one day I may stand before You and hear You say, "Well done, you didn't just 'get through it'... you truly were "salt" and "light" to the next generation" (Matthew 5:13-16).

Claim Your Gold

Application Guide

Engrave your heart:

(Memorize, or simply re-read during the day.)

"... ***Get ready****... Be strong... Be very courageous...*
Meditate on My words, day and night"... Carefully obey...
Do not be discouraged..." -Joshua 1:2-9
"You are the ***salt*** *of the earth.*
But if salt loses its saltiness... it is no longer good for anything...
You are the ***light*** *of the world...*
Let your light shine before men, that they may see your good deeds and praise your Father in heaven." -Matthew 5:13-16 (NIV)

Refine the gold:

Brain studies are now making it possible for the medical, and academic communities to truly focus on rethinking medical treatment and teaching methods. As scientists discover, and learn to understand, brain activity under differing circumstances, doctors are developing medical protocols that leave traditional thinking far behind.

Educators are instituting "brain-based" learning methods that prepare students to become "learning magnets." Recent studies on brain development continue to confirm a theory we've known all along—the importance of the family's role in the early training and education of their children.

Every experience in language and life that the pre-school-age child (or anyone) attains will become a mental "magnet" for future information on the same, or related topic (See figures 1 and 2 on the following page). Students who have been prepared with a bank of "magnets" tend to more easily accumulate expanded knowledge. When a child's "magnet bank" has been limited by lack of preparation, teachers must invest precious time generating preparedness.

This gives us all hope! The more "mental magnets" we've accumulated, the easier it is to learn something new, assuming we are willing to move away from the well-worn cliché, "You can't teach an old dog new tricks," and move on to our true potential. No one has more "mental magnets" then the average golden-ager!

Another benefit of learning how a brain collects information, starting with a tiny seed of truth, is that many of us will become an integral part of a child's (grandkids and others) life. We will have the time to invest in planting those seeds of activity and knowledge that will be "learning magnets" for the rest of their lives. We have been given a mighty task! We must not "just get through" those times we are called to baby-sit. We must carefully prepare our lives to be the role models and teachers God has called us to be.

Reading research on brain-based learning has become a very exciting pastime for me, but I became extremely aware of the concept of "mental magnets" in a very simple way. While purchasing a silver-grey car I thought how easy it was going to be to find it in a parking lot among a rainbow of colors.

After shopping one day, I confidently headed toward the car. As my eye surveyed the parking lot I viewed a sea of silver-grey. My brain had never thought about silver-grey. Now, that is all I could see! Everywhere I went my "silver-grey brain magnet" collected more and more silver-grey. My awareness had been raised.

What's the point?

The Bible made it clear in Matthew 13:12-13, when Jesus said, "Whoever has will be given more... Whoever does not have, even what he has will be taken from him.... Though seeing, they do not see; though hearing they do not hear or understand."

This brings to mind two old sayings we've all heard, and probably said, many times in the past. "Use it, or lose it!" and "A journey of a thousand miles begins with a single step."

Figure 1: Low mental stimulation reduces understanding and insight.

Figure 2: Increased mental stimulation strengthens understanding and insights.

We are embarking on an exciting, all-the-pieces-are-coming-together journey. God has prepared us with thousands of "mental magnets" (single steps) during our past good times and bad times. We have plenty to build on. Now, we must follow the commands God gave to Joshua as he faced the journey to the Promised Land. We must get ready, obey, be strong, and most of all, fill our God-given mental capacity with His Word.

Our success, or failure, in pleasing God is directly determined by the faith we have in the truth of Scripture. If we try to manipulate the words and force them into our way of thinking to justify our actions and words, our faith is weak, or dead! If, however, we can truly say (with Abel, Enoch, Noah, Abraham, Sarah, Isaac, Jacob, Joseph, Moses, Joshua, Rahab, and hundreds of others -Hebrews 11) that we have faith, and obedience, because "God is GOD," and "God said it,...therefore, it is true," then we can be assured that God will lead us and ***never*** forsake us.

A true faith in God's Word takes things promised by Him and transports them into our present situation. We will be infused through the Holy Spirit with spiritual strength, courage, endurance, perseverance, love, joy, peace, light and salt, and we won't "just get through it," we will truly be pleasing to Him!

1. Ask God to confirm your faith, or lack of faith, in His Word.
2. Diligently seek to build on the faith you have. Ask Him to guide you.
3. Research "faith" passages in the Scriptures. Start with Hebrews 11 and 1 John 5:1-5.
4. Meditate on these Scriptures, and how they attest to the value of living by faith.
5. Start a daily "Gratitude Journal."

   Begin by reviewing the activities of your day.

   Determine one thing for which you are the most thankful.

   Record your thankful thoughts along with the date.

   Add a sentence to explain why you thank God for this.

Make an entry every day, even through days of trial. (Ask God to help you maintain a thankful spirit; looking always to a future hope.)

6. Encourage others to gain a heart of thanksgiving.
7. Be salt and light to your world planting "seeds" of faith.
8. When you thank God for a particular person He has placed in your life, take a moment and write a note thanking them for their friendship, their love, their faithfulness to God, etc.
9. Write a note of thanksgiving to your pastor, and other spiritual leaders.
10. When appropriate (Thanksgiving Day, etc.), write a letter to the editor of your local newspaper, reminding readers of God's abundant blessings. (Be a leader in the positive; God's goodness.)
11. Thank Him for the faith He has given you, and the privilege to share it.

"But without faith it is impossible to please Him,
for he who comes to God must believe that ***He IS****,*
and that He is a Rewarder of those who diligently seek Him."
–Hebrews 11:6

Nuggets of wisdom, promises and praise:
(Sing, or simply read as prayerful poetry.)

"Tis So Sweet to Trust in Jesus" by Louisa M. R. Stead

"Tis so sweet to trust in Jesus, Just to take Him at His word,
Just to rest upon His promise, Just to know "Thus saith the Lord."
Refrain:
Jesus, Jesus, how I love Him! How I've proved Him o'er and o'er!
Jesus, Jesus, precious Jesus! O for grace to trust Him more!

O how sweet to trust in Jesus, Just to trust His cleansing blood,
Just in simple faith to plunge me 'Neath the healing, cleansing flood!
Refrain:
Jesus, Jesus, how I love Him! How I've proved Him o'er and o'er!
Jesus, Jesus, precious Jesus! O for grace to trust Him more!

Yes, 'tis sweet to trust in Jesus, Just from sin and self to cease,
Just from Jesus simply taking Life and rest and joy and peace.
Refrain:
Jesus, Jesus, how I love Him! How I've proved Him o'er and o'er!
Jesus, Jesus, precious Jesus! O for grace to trust Him more!

I'm so glad I learned to trust Him, Precious Jesus, Savior, Friend;
And I know that He is with me, Will be with me to the end.
Refrain:
Jesus, Jesus, how I love Him! How I've proved Him o'er and o'er!
Jesus, Jesus, precious Jesus! O for grace to trust Him more!

Chapter 14

"Think Outside the Box"

Grow in God's Grace

maximize, v.- 1. to increase to the greatest possible amount or degree.
2. to make fullest use of.

If we choose to follow Christ and glorify Him with our actions, lips and hearts, we must prepare. We must decide how to maximize the capacity of the "box" God has put us into. The "box" of being human is created the minute we enter the arena of time, space, and gravity. These are our boundaries! They help to determine our *capacity* for fulfilling God's given purpose for our lives, which is to—

*"**Love** the LORD your God*
with all your heart, with all your soul, and with all our mind...
*and you shall **love** your neighbor as yourself."*
-Matthew 22:37-39

Jesus, Himself, took on the limitations of time, space and gravity in order to identify with us, and exemplify the use of this "box." His space was limited to about 60 square miles (Israel), His time confined to 33 years, and the effects of gravity pulled on Him as on us. Compared to our life span, and our freedom to move to all the "corners" of the earth in gravity-defying inventions, Christ's earthly "box" was tiny. As small as it was He was able to affect the whole world for all time and all eternity. People were drawn to His space. He knew what He needed to do with every minute of His time, and He didn't bodily fly around defying gravity—He walked. He used His humanness to show us effective methods for "thinking outside the box."

The capacity of Abraham's faith-filled "box" also extends to all the corners of the earth, and through all generations. Unfortunately, the God-honoring capacity of his nephew Lot's "box" became quite small when his family found it hard to follow his lead. Miriam's "box" shrank the minute she decided to put herself above God's will.

On the other hand, Ruth's boundaries expanded when she decided, not only to stay with her mother-in-law, Naomi, but also to seek and follow Naomi's God (Ruth 1:16). It's possible that Ruth, the great-grandmother of King David, was the model for the description of the wife of Proverb's 31. Ruth was devoted to her family (Ruth 1:15-18), diligent in her labor (Ruth 2:7, 17, 23), dependent on God (Ruth 2:12), and filled with many other Proverbs 31 character traits. Her "box" could have shrunk dramatically if she had simply gone home to her people and their gods, and had fallen into the narrow "box" of a lowly widow.

Joshua's "space" increased 100?… 1000?… fold when he displayed his trust in God, and his desire to obey (Numbers 14:6-9). At age 90 he followed in the footsteps of Moses, and led the Children of Israel as they conquered the "space" of the Promised Land.

Christ's character, His truth, and His principles for a God-honoring life are carefully recorded for us on the pages of the Bible. Hebrews 13:8 assures us that "Jesus Christ is the same yesterday, today and forever." His promises stand for ancient Israel as well as for our present world, and through all eternity.

God has used the "backdrop" of the lives of many men and woman to illuminate the way He is able to work through obedient, willing saints. He *never* changes! (Hebrews 13:8). He is never inconsistent. The purpose of the Scriptures is to give us hope, and show us how to please God. Times, places and people have changed, but not God. His character and His truth remain the same through *all* generations. He is our Rock, Anchor, Savior and loving, compassionate Father and Friend, and He has a plan for the time and space He provides for each of us.

With only our wisdom and our strength, our "box" will become smaller and smaller as the years go by. Our time will become limited as the years slip away, and the space we are able to cover will shrink when our physical abilities diminish. Gravity will become the bane of our existence. Not only will it pull us down, but, if we let it, it will cause us too much effort to get up and keep moving. Soon we will be like that diamond, in our little dusty "box," sitting on the "jeweler's" shelf, grumbling and complaining about having no purpose. We will undoubtedly be there with many, many other dusty "boxes," not even able, or willing, to show God's beauty to each other.

We've heard it said, *"Think outside the box!"... "Think outside the box!"* Romans 12:2 tells us to **renew our minds** and not conform to thinking the way the world thinks in their little "boxes" (*comfort zones*).

God ***is*** outside the "box!" God is also inside the "box!" God is "there;" He is *omnipresent*, everywhere at the same time. If we truly desire to obey God and listen to Solomon's wisdom to plan "now," the capacity for glorifying and reflecting His magnificence will be greater than when we were young.

"I must decrease; He must increase."
-John 3:30

Do we fear old age? God tells us in Psalm 2:11, 25:12-14, Ecclesiastes 12:13 that we are to fear being unfaithful to Him. On the other hand, we are instructed over and over again not to fear (Psalm 27:1, 3, 14, 112:7), and not to worry (Matthew 6:25-34), and not to fret (Psalm 37:1, 7, 8).

One of my favorite illustrations that Jesus used to explain what God desires from us in the area of faithfulness and obedience is the parable of the "talents" in Matthew 25:14-30.

"Talents" are not coins. A talent was a measure of weight. It could be translated as an amount of money, or as this parable suggests, a natural gift or ability. (We all have the gift of a God-measured amount of time and space.)

The parable illustrates the tragedy of wasted opportunity. Three servants are given differing numbers of talents according to their abilities (Matt. 25:15). They are asked to be good stewards of what they were given. This represents the "box" we have been given. It symbolizes the specific time, space, and strength against gravity that God has given us, and all our other skills, and gifts, as well.

In the story, the two servants who were faithful to the task were successful in producing "fruit" to one degree or another. They both received the same reward. The owner congratulated them with, "Well done." He told them that since they were faithful in the way they handled a few things, he was going to make them rulers over many things. (They increased the capacity of their "boxes!")

Christ balances the parable with the negative, and answers the "What if…" question. What if we have a talent and we let time get away from us, or we get lazy and let gravity pull us to a lethargic stand still? What if we fearfully hide our talent? The Bible makes it clear! The servant who buried his talent made excuses, and actually blamed his master for his lack of success. What an incredible way to infuriate your master! The talent was removed from the control of the slothful servant, and given to someone who would be faithful. (Use it, or lose it!)

That is *not* the end of the story! It was obvious the last "servant" was a hypocrite. He was unable to accept the truth of his own decision. He would not take responsibility for his unfaithfulness, and he was cast into outer darkness (Matt. 25:30).

The earthly "box" we inhabit includes time, space and gravity. Faithful stewards who use these "talents" wisely and productively will increase the size of their "box," and be graced by God with an inheritance of immeasurable blessings.

But how can we increase our time? The Bible says we can't add even a moment to the time we've been allotted (Matt. 6:27). And space? How could we find more space… and gravity?

Many of our God-given talents and, more importantly, our faith in the Scriptures and the indwelling of the Holy Spirit, will help us expand these areas. Efficient time management, active living and the art of true hospitality will maximize our lives. If we don't feel especially gifted in any or all of these talents, more glory will go to God when we seek His help. The Holy Spirit empowered Christ's apostles to expand their "boxes" to the "ends of the earth" (Acts 1:8). The same Holy Spirit is within every believer.

Ephesians 5:18 says, "Be filled with the Spirit." In order to be filled with the Spirit rather than be filled with ourselves, we must lay down our life (Rom. 12:1), and yield our will to the control of the Spirit. If we have enough self-control to take that first step of faith, the Holy Spirit will fill us with fruitfulness. We will reflect the character of God in love, joy, peace, kindness, goodness, gentleness, and patience. We will also be overwhelmed with the need to be faithful, and the power of increased self-control. The more control we give up, the more power He gives us. Beautiful things will begin to happen!

Our hearts, will soar (above the effects of gravity), and sing with joy. We will spend our time rejoicing, and words of gratitude and thanksgiving will flow from our lips.

When someone enters our space, our kind and gentle manner will reward us with loving relationships. Others will be drawn to our space, and the sweetness of our attitude will cause their hearts to be lifted above their cares, and they will take time to rejoice and thank God.

Through the mouths and hearts of others the capacity of our "box" will balloon to unimaginable proportions, and the glory to God will be magnified. (Psalm 34:3)

Bob Vernon retired from the Los Angeles Police Department after 37 years on the job (God's training for a bigger capacity for service). He was in line to become Chief, but charges were trumped up against him. His adversaries claimed, in the press (front page), that he only promoted Christians, and that he required those who sought promotion to attend his church. Of course, none of this was true! Even though he was exonerated (in the back pages of the newspaper), someone else was promoted to Chief of the LAPD.

How could this be? He had lived a God-honoring life. He admits to questioning God's goodness and fairness. He thought his "box" was wrapped up, but to his questioning prayers God answered in a most unexpected way. He put him into a "box" with a much larger capacity. More lives would be touched for eternity.

God has taken Bob around the world to train top leaders in the Christian ethics and philosophy of leadership. He has conducted seminars for military, police, and political leaders in over 30 countries. And since hearing of his success with foreign governments, even our own FBI is seeking his wisdom and instruction.

God has expanded Bob's sphere of influence (his "box") because of his passionate desire, obedience, and commitment to maximizing his life for God's glory.

When we are willing to "super-size" our influence for the glory of God, and not ourselves, He will show us exactly how to proceed.

Many of us are saying, "But I'm no Bob Vernon. I don't have that kind of training." This leads me to my next example of a faithful follower maximizing the influence of her life.

She was a mom with a heart for her own children, and also, the children of her community. She volunteered one afternoon a week to teach in an after-school Good News club. Children would come from the local schools to hear about Jesus. She faithfully taught the message of the "Bridge of Christ," and gave the children the opportunity to respond.

Through the years, this faithful woman prayed for each and every child, by name, each and every day. She never knew the results of God's work in most of their lives, but she continued her prayers for them until her death in her late 90s.

During her prayer time each day she would open an old, tattered and taped See's Candy box and, one by one, remove fading pictures of precious lives she had led to the Lord so many years before. She had carefully recorded their names and addresses on the back of each photograph.

One day her dimming eyes caught the headline of the local newspaper. She saw a name she remembered, but was unsure if it was the "Bobby" she had led to the Lord, and was now praying for every day. Her gnarled hands shook as she dialed the number of the police station. Would he remember her, and agree to meet with her?

Bob Vernon certainly remembered her, and with his assigned driver/bodyguard, went to visit. As the door opened he saw familiar twinkling eyes peering through the wrinkles of a 90-year-old face. The two men slowly followed as she cautiously maneuvered her "walker" to the kitchen table. Bob saw the tattered "prayer box," and watched her carefully withdraw his yellowed picture. He could tell she had touched it many times, and his hope swelled as her humble life encouraged him to, "look past this present situation, and keep your eyes on the true goal, and purpose for your life."

As Bob and his burly bodyguard reached the car, their eyes met, and with tears running down his face, his driver softly voiced the desire of his heart: *"I wish someone was praying for me."*

We all know numerous people who would cherish our daily prayers for their lives. The time we spend watching one TV show everyday (or something equivalent), could be set aside and dedicated to "super-sizing" our prayer lives. Think of the number of hearts we could encourage through the power of the Holy Spirit. Encouraged hearts lead to lips that praise and thank the source of their strength—all mighty God.

As we infect others to honor and glorify our LORD, a contagious chain reaction begins, and we will fulfill our earthly purpose of praising God and loving our neighbor enough to cause them to also praise God and love their neighbor into praising God.

In the process, as we focus our self-control on using our time more efficiently and productively, we will spend more minutes, hours, days and years singing with joy and praying in contented peace. As we adjust our attitudes to see God as the provider of all we have, we will thank Him for *all* things (1 Thes. 5:16-18).

If we truly thank Him for everything, we will hardly have time for anything else. But God promises that if we seek Him first (Matt.

6:33), and think on good things (Phil. 4:8), He will free up time and resources for all the other things *He* wants for us.

It is so uplifting to be around someone who is kind, encouraging, and patient. And how soothing to be in the presence of someone who seeks God's wisdom and insights, and then communicates them lovingly and gently, with a heart of passion and care.

Oh, to be that person!

A kind and gentle Spirit, praising God and encouraging others—what else do we need? Our shaky limbs, dim eyes and all the other evil things of Solomon's litany, will pale in comparison. People will be drawn to our space, and as we infect them with our joy, they in turn, will praise God, and infect someone else.

When we cause others to *soar* above the gravity of their weighty worldly woes, we touch the very heart of God, and God smiles and our purpose here is not only fulfilled…it is **MAXIMIZED**!

O Father,

I thank You for the time You have given me on earth. I pray that You will teach me to maximize it by being more efficient. Touch my memory, and help me to remember Your faithfulness to me. I may forget everything else, but never let me forget to be thankful.

Fill my space with people. Like Stephen, let them see Your beauty on my face (Acts 6:15), *in my eyes, and through my positive and contented attitude.*

Carry me on Your Wings, and let me flourish and soar higher every day. Let me see the smile on Your Face as my-world magnifies Your Holy Name.

I pray that my last day here will be my best day here!

When You whisk me to Your Presence may I hear You say, "Well done, you were known to be full of Spirit, and wisdom (Acts 6:3). *You didn't bury the talents, time and space I gave you, and you've soared into My Heart."*

Claim Your Gold

Application Guide

Engrave your heart:

(Memorize, or simply re-read during the day.)

"Be very careful, then, how you live—not as the unwise but as wise,
making the most of every opportunity..."
-Ephesians 5:15 (NIV)

"Therefore, do not be unwise,
but understand what the will of the LORD is."
-Ephesians 5:17

"...be filled with the Spirit...always giving thanks to God the Father
for everything, in the Name of our LORD Jesus Christ."
-Ephesians 5:18 & 20

Refine the gold:

As newborn babies enter the realm of time, space, and gravity, any parent can tell you these tiny creatures will have only one thing on their agendas—me, myself and I. There is no thought of dad and mom's comfort or lack of sleep. "I want what I want when I want it, and I want it ***now***!" No one needs to be taught how to be self-centered. It comes as standard operating equipment.

The job of the parents, family, the church, the school and society in general is to train these selfish creatures to think beyond themselves.

Most every culture has some form of the Golden Rule—*"Do unto others as you would have them do unto you."* We all must learn to fit in and get along.

As our lives expand to include family, friends, work associates and others, our self-centeredness needs to either be put aside, or be "masked" enough to give us some semblance of maturity. One way or the other, we witness the Golden Rule in action.

Then the course of our lives changes; an empty nest, retirement, health problems, etc., decrease our contact with other people. Our need for the Golden Rule seems to diminish. We spend most of our time and energy on our own needs. Our new Golden Rule could easily become, *"Do unto myself as I would have others do unto me."*

This is the path of human nature. As our "box" shrinks, our focus tends to shrink also. And yet the Bible reminds us—*"I must decrease; He* (all His characteristics) *must increase"* (John 3:30).

A visual of "life" could fit into various "boxes," but for the sake of this illustration I have pictured the life of the "natural" man in three boxes; also the life of the "Spirit filled" man. (See Figures 1-4 on following pages.)

1. Carefully consider the illustrations on the next four pages.
2. Put yourself into Box #3 for "Growing Down." (Figure 1)
3. Discuss with a close friend, journal, or simply think about what *you* look like when you are "walking" in this mode. (We all do at times.)
4. List all the positives you display to God while operating in this way (are there any?)—list the negatives.
5. Ask the LORD to make you sensitive to your own "walk."
6. Now, put yourself into Box #3 of "Growing Up." (Figure 2)
7. Discuss how you can make this a reality in your life, 24/7.
8. Thank God for the power of the Holy Spirit. (view Figures 3 & 4)
9. ***Today***, find one person that you can influence, and/or encourage to **thank, praise, glorify** and **magnify** God's most precious Name.

NATURAL
"MAN"
grows down
NOT UP!

BOX #1-Childhood
me-myself-I

BOX #2-Adult Responsibilities
Care
for
Others

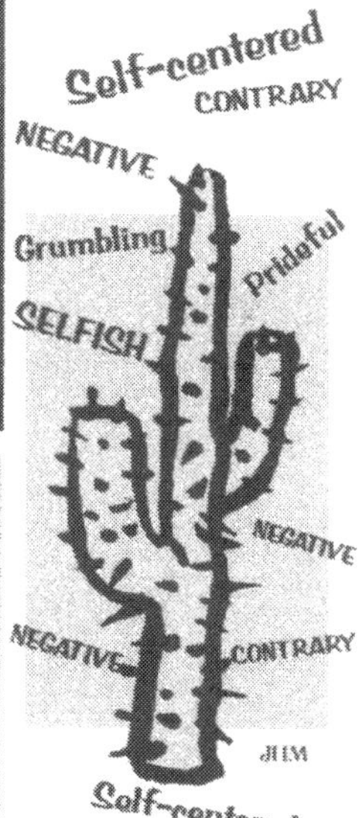
Self-centered
CONTRARY
NEGATIVE
Grumbling
Prideful
SELFISH
NEGATIVE
NEGATIVE
CONTRARY
Self-centered
Grumbling

I want
what I want...
and I want it
NOW!!!

BOX #3-Old Age
me-myself-I

Figure 1

Spirit filled "man"

"The righteous shall flourish like a palm tree...
They shall still bear fruit in old age." Psalm 92:12-14

WHICH WILL BE YOUR LEGACY?

Jeremiah 17:5-8

Figure 3

Which will MAGNIFY God's Character?
LOVE
JOY
LIGHT
LOVE
ETERNAL
GOLDEN
PEACE
JUSTICE
"COME"
"I Love You!"
OR
JHM

Figure 4

Nuggets of wisdom, promises and praise:
(Sing, or simply read as prayerful poetry.)

"All For Jesus" by Mary D. James

All for Jesus, all for Jesus! All my being's ransomed pow'rs:
All my thoughts and all my doings, All my days and all my hours.
All for Jesus, all for Jesus! All my days and all my hours;
All for Jesus, all for Jesus! All my days and all my hours.

Let my hands perform His biding, Let my feet run in His ways;
Let my eyes see Jesus only, Let my lips speak forth His praise.
All for Jesus, all for Jesus! Let my lips speak forth His praise.
All for Jesus, all for Jesus! Let my lips speak forth His praise.

Oh, what wonder! How amazing! Jesus, glorious King of kings,
Deigns to call me His beloved, Lets me rest beneath His wings.
All for Jesus, all for Jesus! Resting now beneath His wings.
All for Jesus, all for Jesus! Resting now beneath His wings.

Chapter 15
Examine Yourself
Use God's Scorecard

examine, v.- 1. to inspect or scrutinized carefully.
2. to test knowledge,
reactions or qualifications.
truth, n.- the true or actual state of a matter.

When we listen to "negative press" (the "wisdom" of the world) that subtly, and not so subtly, erodes our confidence as we face our "declining" years, we become ineffective victims. The culture gives up on us, and we, in turn, may even give up on ourselves. Many seniors citizens just shutdown! They stop "growing" and moving forward. They lose any sense of hope, and purpose.

When any of us are not moving forward, striving toward a goal, we stand still. Eventually, others pass us by, and not only does it seem as if we are going backwards, we actually start to regress.

As advances in technology make it possible to unlock some of the secrets of brain activity for all age groups, current studies confirm what the Word of God told us in the very beginning…we are "fearfully and wonderfully made…" (Psalm 139:14). However, if we don't keep examining ourselves, through all stages of our lives, we will lose our focus and our hope. We will give in to popular "wisdom" that tells us again and again that old age is the cause and the blame for many of our new challenges. We may even succumb to the notion that we have no purpose. Once we let that thinking invade our minds, we lose our hope!

When hope is gone, the motivation to fulfill our God-given purpose evaporates, and those "difficult days" of Ecclesiastes 12:1 penetrate our every thought. We then have two choices. We can either, "lie down and roll over" in complete helplessness, or we can seek God's presence, strength, power and purpose in our despair, and through Him, soar to new heights.

At all stages of life the choice is ours! That is our gift from God—free will.

The first step, at any stage of life, is always to examine where we stand. The only way we can truly see where we are, and *not* where we think we are, is to ask God, through the power of the Holy Spirit, to lead us in truth. Anything less will produce skewed results that will mislead us into thinking we are someone other than the person God knows we really are. We know this as self-righteous thinking.

What a disaster it would be if we "cheated" on the test of self-examination, and built our beautiful, religious-looking "house" on this sandy foundation (Matt. 7:26-27).

If we don't examine ourselves in truth, and in view of God's terms for a life of righteous obedience, we forfeit the blessings prepared for us. We will become the "fool" of so many of God's proverbs (Prov. 12:23, 15, 16; 11:22; 13:19).

By pulling Christ-like characteristics from the Word of God we can put together a basic checklist for examination purposes. In the "good old days" we looked forward to Report Card day with a sense of confidence, or a horrifying fear of the truth. If we truly wanted to succeed on the next report card, we learned to seek help, and work hard to overcome our failures. There were also those who accepted their fate as already sealed, and just gave up.

It is never, *ever*, too late to grow in the LORD, through His power, as long as our breath lingers, and our minds retain even a shed of desire. Our first desire must be to assess our character in truth as God, and others see us.

Our "Report Card" might look something like this:

(insert your name)'s actions show he/she is **consistently**:

* loving with all people.(John 13:35)
  Yes___ No___
* kind…gentle… patient (Gal. 5:22-23)
  Yes___ No___
* has an overwhelming desire to read, or listen to God's Word, and submits to it (II Tim. 2:15)
  Yes___ No___
* loves "neighbors" (Matt. 5:43)
  Yes___ No___
* loves enemies, and prays for them (Matt. 5:44)
  Yes___ No___
* speaks lovingly in truth (Matt. 12:34)
  Yes___ No___
* gives of time, and resources, without craving public recognition (Matt. 6:1-4)
  Yes___ No___
* "works" well with everyone (Matt. 7:1-12)
  Yes___ No___
* seeks God's will on a daily basis (Matt. 5:6)
  Yes___ No___
* has a passionate desire to be like Christ (1 Cor. 2:6-16)
  Yes___ No___

Of course, the key word in the scoring process is "consistently." Because none of us are God, we will never be perfect in any of these areas. But, if our true desire is to follow Christ's example, our actions, our attitudes and our words will become more and more consistent with His righteousness.

In order to truthfully score a "Yes" in all the areas we must be "walking" in the strength and power of the Holy Spirit. No human has the resources within themselves to live up to God's Holy standards. In Matthew 19:25-26, Christ tells us, "With men this is impossible, but with God, all things are possible."

There it is! GOD is our hope! He is faithful to His promises. Our purpose is continually defined for us throughout the Scriptures.

Joshua (22:5 -NIV) says:

1. "Love the LORD your God."
2. "Walk in His ways."
3. "Obey His commands."
4. "Hold fast to Him."
5. "Serve Him with all your heart and soul."

This is echoed in Mark 12:30-31 with the addition of:

6. "Love your neighbor as yourself."

When we know we are indeed His disciples, our hope is complete. Our next task is to examine our definition of "love, kindness, gentleness, goodness," and all the other words we are asked to display (Gal. 5:22-23).

Our opinion of "kindness" and "gentleness" will be based, in most part, on what we have experienced from others—an encouraging smile, a kind word, a gentle tone or touch. Unfortunately, some of us may never have experienced any measure of true kindness or gentleness, but we are not exempt! How, then, will we show these Godly qualities to the next generation if we have never seen them modeled? How will we know what they "look like"?

Many people are absolutely unable to mouth, much less verbalize the words, "I love you"…"I cherish you"…"I need you." They were brought up without the privilege of hearing these words related to themselves. They could just leave it at that, and blame their upbringing, or they could make a plan to learn to express their love, their thankfulness and their compassion.

I know it can be done because I was one of those people. Being shy in the first place, it was already hard for me to speak, but to say something as important as "I love you" was more than impossible! For some reason (The Holy Spirit, you think?) I felt pressure from inside me to conquer this. I asked the LORD to show me how. I started by telling Him I loved Him, but I only said it in my mind! I then decided to write short prayers in a journal, and end each prayer with "I love You." I moved on to softly (reading) whispering my prayers out loud during my quite time, and hearing my own voice verbalize the words.

Each step took me to the next until I actually caught myself walking through the market praising God in my mind, for something that had happened during the day, and with my eyes on my shopping cart and without thinking I audibly said, "I love you!" Just as I said it, I glanced up into the eyes of a passing shopper. We both gave a nervous laugh, and I quickly explained that I had been praying, and I was so involved I hadn't realized I was praying out loud. He said, "I love Him, too!" As he walked away I realized how much I had changed. Months earlier I had trouble even thinking the words without blushing, and now I'm telling the world (Psalm 49:1).

I then made plans for telling my world how much I love them. Would they laugh? Would they faint? It was a risk I wanted to take. I know that when I'm able to express my ideas, thoughts and feelings in words, they become more concrete.

My world didn't laugh or faint! They each looked a little taken back, but because I was able to say it, they in turn took the risk. They each told me how much they loved me. Wow! What a pay-off!

Those words are not to be taken lightly. They are not just another way of saying "goodbye." They are precious gifts we give each other—gifts that grow in our hearts and create an overwhelming thankfulness to God.

Three little words… eight little letters (great song title!) have changed the whole tone and focus of our home. We always knew we loved each other, but until I examined myself, and discovered my part in holding us back, we never moved forward. Anyone of us could have broken the silence. It only takes one spark to create a warm, inviting fire! I want to be that spark!

O Father,

Thank You for being the spark in my life. Thank You for fanning the flames and igniting my passion for You. I love You so! I pray that You will love the people on my path through me. Help me to display Your kindness, gentleness, goodness and love to them. Let me cause them to cry out to You in joy for the love they feel. Let my love, patience and peace increase with every passing day.

May I one day stand before You, and hear You say, "Well done... you examined yourself in My Light, and saturated your life in My Word." (Psalm 26:2, John 8:31-32)

Claim Your Gold

Application Guide

Engrave your heart:
(Memorize, or simply re-read during the day.)

"Examine me, O LORD, and ***prove me****;*
Try my mind and my heart."
-Psalm 26:2

"If you abide in My Word, you are My disciples indeed.
And you shall know the ***truth****, and the truth shall make you free."*
-John 8:31-32

Refine the gold:

The key word to any examination is "truth." If we don't walk in truth, we will be walking in false hopes and denial.

This was brought home to me in a very powerful way the year I had to renew my health status for the Board of Education. I made an appointment with the Board doctor, instead of my own doctor, knowing that the paperwork would have a better chance of getting to my records, and not being lost in transit.

When I arrived in his office, the doctor who had given me my first health exam, 30 years before, met me. I felt confident! I knew he had many years of experience. My confidence soon turned to dismay when he couldn't find his glasses, and he couldn't remember the answers I gave him as he asked me if I was healthy. At the end of the interview he signed my form (I had to point to the line for his signature), and

I was happily on my way. I *knew* I was healthy, but I just needed someone else to confirm it.

Unfortunately, I hadn't asked the right doctor to examine me, for it was during that school year that my cancer was eventually discovered. I was walking, all those months, in false hope. I could have been seeking early treatment that would have not allowed the disease to penetrate my lymph system.

As we transfer this experience to examining our personal spiritual condition we must never walk in denial. If we think we are flawless, we have deceived ourselves. Eventually (when life gets out of our control), the Light of truth will illuminate our character flaws. Our world will see things and hear words coming from our lips that will completely undermine our self-righteous life. The truth that God sees in our heart will escape our lips, and our "cover will be blown."

Our only hope lies in God's willingness to help us clean our heart, and fill it with all the fruit of His Spirit, when we see our need, desire a true change, and ***ask***. Then, during our last days, when we may only have the use of our lips, God's love, kindness, gentleness, goodness, (Can you name all the fruit of the Spirit, yet?) etc., will flow freely, 24/7, from our lips.

The first test of physical healthiness is obvious to even the most incompetent physician. Is the patient alive? If not, there is no need to go forward with the examination. The same is true for our spiritual lives. Are we spiritually alive through the Bridge of Christ? Without that path to God, the power of the Holy Spirit is not available to us.

Once we've established our life in Christ, it's time to determine if we're "walking" in our own strength, or the strength, wisdom, insights and understanding of the Holy Spirit. We must examine our words, and actions.

1. Plan to examine yourself on a regular basis—"Am I Spiritually alive? Am I continuing to seek God's will for my life even though others keep pointing to my physical challenges of aging? Do I have a desire, and passion to make my last day on earth my best day in Christ?"

2. Ask God to keep you faithful to the truth.

3. Know the truth by ***saturating your mind with Scripture***.

4. Ask God to reveal your weaknesses, which might include:
   – self-righteousness, pride and/or arrogance.
   – hypocritical words that don't match your actions.
   – selfishness and self-centeredness.
   – laziness and/or unfaithfulness.
   – poor use of time and/or resources.
   – a manipulative lack of truthfulness.
   – a critical, impatient and/or harsh, judgmental spirit.
   – negativity, grumbling and/or complaining.
   – an unloving, unkind and/or inconsiderate attitude.
   – divisive and/or meddling behavior.
   – joyless, grumbling ungratefulness.
   – quarrelsome, argumentative and/or angry attitude.
   – a pouter, or a user of "adult" temper tantrums.
   – blame shifting and denial.
   – holier-than-thou prideful attitude.
   – unforgiving and/or hateful spirit.
   – gossiping and/or jealousy.

5. Ask God's forgiveness, and yield your will to His terms.

6. Watch your life make a 180-degree turn, and ***praise God*** always.

Nuggets of wisdom, promises and praise:
(Sing, or simply read as prayerful poetry.)

"Breathe on Me, Breath of God" by Edwin Hatch

Breathe on me, Breath of God, Fill me with life anew,
That I may love what Thou dost love, And do what Thou would do.

Breathe on me, Breath of God, Until my heart is pure,
Until my will is one with Thine, To do and to endure.

Breathe on me, Breath of God, Till I am wholly Thine,
Until this earthly part of me Glows with Thy fire divine.

Chapter 16
Foolproof Your Life
Saturate Your Mind with God's Word

read, v.- 1. to look at so as to understand
the meaning of something written or printed.
2. to interpret meaning.
3. to infer.
4. to discover
5. to obtain knowledge.

The Scriptures say (Matt. 6:5-6) that we are not to pray in a showy way, but we are to go into our closet to pray. I'm afraid if I did that I would get distracted, and start to reorganize, so I put myself in a "closet" where I know I will be able to focus. My kitchen table in the early morning is my "closet."

Years ago one of my very foolish habits was to "multi-task" everything. And as I came before God's Throne during my "quiet" time my mind would be running wild with thoughts of the day.

I knew that if Christ were physically sitting across the table from me, the rest of the world would disappear, and I would be engulfed in His words, wisdom and insights. Having Him at my table is a scene I've wished for all my life!

In my early years as a "non-Scripture reading" Christian, I foolishly looked at the Bible as an old-fashioned, hard-to-read book. I was happy to just let each pastor of wherever I was attending church at the time fill me in on what he thought I should know. Oh, maybe I would read a few verses now and then or use one of those quickie little devotional books, because I knew I was supposed to. I figured if anyone asked if I read my Bible I could say, "Why yes, don't you?"

Many years ago I was following this hit-and-miss Bible "study plan" and fooling myself into thinking I was doing it right. I could not understand why my life, and the life of my family, was in such distress. With all my energy and pride I worked night and day to straighten out the mess, and try to find the peace and joy that I had only heard about. What was wrong with me? Why couldn't I succeed? Where was God? I asked Him every day to bless my efforts. I knew the Bible said "ask" (It was right there in my little devotional book!), so I asked. Not only that, I asked "in Jesus' Name." What more could I do?

I finally came to a moment in time when I asked the Lord to take me "home" to heaven, because it seemed I was only making things worse rather than better. He confirmed my theory. In my heart I knew I was right! *I* was the problem! I needed to surrender my prideful heart, ask the LORD for forgiveness, and seek *His* will for the next step.

When I realized I had no more options except to surrender to His wisdom, I decided to do some serious research. I wouldn't take anyone's word for what the Scriptures say. I would use my own God-given talent! I would ***read***! What a concept! God had allowed me to acquire the skill of reading, and yet, I was living and acting like a person who couldn't read. I was the servant of Matthew 25:24-29 who buried his "talent" and still expected to be blessed.

My first step was to find an easy-to-follow plan for Bible study. "One-size" does not fit all! There were several good plans I came across in my search—I even found some wonderful large print Bibles that I know I will be using one of these days. What worked for me was a Bible that was divided, by date, into daily reading from both the Old and New Testaments. Year-after-year I've read through this Bible, or one like it, and every year the LORD applies it to my life in a different way. The depth of His wisdom is unfathomable! (Psalm 51:6).

As I have matured in my walk with the LORD I've added other components to my "closet" time, such as study Bibles, commentaries, prayer journals, etc. Now, little devotional books are a bonus resource.

My kitchen table has become my early morning meeting place with my LORD. When I first started meeting with Him there, I would spend 10 or 15 minutes reading, and then a couple of minutes jotting down a one or two sentence prayer in my journal. I always wondered if anyone ever filled up all that space they gave you to write a daily prayer.

Now, I spend an hour or more with Him every morning. I actually have to limit myself, and/or get up earlier, because I become so "lost" in communication with my Heavenly Father, that at one point I was getting to work later and later every day. Ecclesiastes 3 tells us there is a time for everything, and I knew that what I had learned that morning would be useless if I didn't apply it properly. I had to be on time!

My life, and my family's life, slowly started to move forward.

What a fool I had been! Solomon continually warns us to stay away from fools, because their folly will lead to folly of our own (Prov. 14:7-8). How could I become a "prudent person" who acted out of knowledge and truth, rather than folly (Prov.13:16)? The answer was obvious. Keep reading! Keep seeking, and never forsake God's purpose for my life.

Is that all?

It seemed overwhelming at the time. I had too many self-made problems that were always competing for my attention. But then I noticed my feeling of peace was increasing. The Holy Spirit was working together with my newly found Scriptural input, and my willingness to try to obey. I saw my life begin to change, and it motivated me to delve deeper into God's resources. As I went deeper my focus became clearer, and verses came alive.

*"Seek ye **first** the kingdom of God, and His righteousness,*
and all these things will be added unto you."
-Matthew 6:33

This was becoming a reality in my life! I knew if I just read what was there, and didn't use what I learned, it was all in vain, and a big waste of my time. I had to be willing to examine myself in honesty, and lay down those things in my life (Rom. 12:1) that were displeasing to God.

What were those things? I could see them easily in the lives of others—self-righteousness, hypocritical living, blame shifting, constant complaining, a negative spirit, etc. I asked the LORD to show me. He was so faithful to quickly answering that prayer! Since I truly wanted to know, He led my thinking step-by-step from my prideful attitude to my grumbling—from my blaming to my lack of deep understanding. It was hard! The pressure of change was ever before me. The work will never be finished, but as I learn the blessings of a submitted life I wonder how I ever thought my way was better.

Five years after I started the renewal of my life and my mind (Rom. 12:2), I was faced with an overwhelming diagnosis of cancer. The course of my treatment took me from surgery, to chemo, to radiation and back to chemo. I spent one hairless year in the process, and another year, or so, recovering from the process.

I could not believe my reaction to the whole thing! I wasn't grumbling and complaining. I wasn't blaming God, or the doctors, or trying to deny and avoid this "cup" God had waiting for me. I was at complete peace! Of course I was scared! Were these my last days on earth? Was the LORD answering my earlier prayer, and taking me "home"? Would I not live long enough to see my family re-energized and glorifying God? So many thoughts swirled in my head, and yet, the LORD was holding my heart. The knowledge of His word, that had transformed my thinking, was moving from head knowledge to deep understanding, and trust in His love and compassion for me.

As I would lie awake on my bed, searching for meaning, He was there! He bathed my memory with His promises. Verse after verse came flooding through my mind. He showed me He meant what He said! I came to the place of Paul when he said, "For me to live is Christ, and to die is gain" (Phil. 1:21).

I really didn't care which way God wanted to take me. I was filled with joy about either possibility.

I actually look back on that time with incredible thankfulness. If I hadn't had the opportunity to go through the "slash, burn and poisoning" of cancer treatment, my understanding of God's power would be limited to hearsay. Through the darkness of that year, Christ's glory shone brightly in my life.

My constant prayer is that as I face the coming test of old age, and all its evil attacks on my body, I will continue to examine myself, and submit to God's truth concerning His purpose for me.

O Father,

I thank You for my life! Most of all I Thank You for my new life since You led me to Your "Bridge" of Christ, saved my soul from the dark, lonely "chasm" and filled me with Your Holy Spirit. How do people make it through the evils of this world without You? Your love, compassion and promises for me are my hope (1 Corinthians 13:12-13). *Thank You for prodding me to use my reading skills to discover all Your promises. When my heart and my flesh fail me You are there* (Psalm 73:26). *You hold me in Your tender Hand and cover me with Your warm, soft wing* (Psalm 17:7-8, 36:7). *How can I thank You in a more appropriate way? My words are meager, and cannot fully express my love and gratitude for Your constant caring. I love You, LORD! You are my strength and my heart!* (Psalm 18:1).

May I one day stand before You and hear You say the words I feel each day... "I love You, my precious servant, come into My Arms." (Psalm 116:15-16).

Claim Your Gold

Application Guide

Engrave your heart:
(Memorize, or simply re-read during the day.)

"Every prudent "man" acts out of
***knowledge**, But a fool exposes his folly."*
-Proverbs 13:16 (NIV)

"Blessed is the "man" who does not walk in the counsel of the wicked,
or stand in the way of sinners or sit in the seat of mockers.
But *his delight is in the law of the LORD,*
and on His law he ***meditates*** *day and night.* -Psalm 1:1-2 (NIV)

"He is like a tree planted by streams of water, which yields its ***fruit*** *in season*
and whose leaf does not wither. Whatever he does prospers."
-Psalm 1:3 (NIV)

Refine the gold:

I'm always amazed when I listen as self-proclaimed, "educated" people expound on various topics. They seem to have a quick answer for all the world's woes. Every human condition could easily be remedied if only things would be handled their way. Most of the input these people have comes from one-minute sound bites from news media, commercials, friends and other "authorities."

I'm sure we can all relate!

When was the last time *we* expounded our "knowledge" on a political, educational, medical, spiritual, or other topic? How much true research had we done on the topic before we passed on someone else's sound bites? Count the number of football, basketball (etc.) teams *we* have brought to victory, before we loudly, and authoritatively, instruct the coach on how it should be done properly.

Dedicated educators know that they can't simply rely on remembering how their teachers taught them. And they can't continue to just do the same old, non-productive lessons, over and over, year after year, if they want to maximize their results in an ever-changing educational climate. This is basically the "bottom line" in any organization; **MAXIMIZE** results.

In order to move forward, and not fall behind, most truly dedicated people will tell you they must read material in their field of expertise for at least 45 minutes a day. Of course, reading isn't everything! Application is the key!

If our true purpose in life is to please God in our words, actions, and, most of all, the motives of our heart, then we can't afford to rely on "Christian" sound bites and false tradition. The only way to maximize our obedience to God's Word is to commit to making this our field of expertise.

Studies show that among those who claim to be "born-again Christians," only about 18% read the Bible on a daily basis. Twenty-three percent confess they ***never*** read the Word of God. The majority of Christians have never read the Bible all the way through.

Viewing the length of the Bible discourages most people. And yet, if we do the math we see that reading a few minutes a day, consistently, will take us through the Bible in one to three years. Tapes and CD recordings of the complete text of the Bible fill 72 hours. Seventy-two hours times 60 minutes for each hour equals 4,320 minutes. Divide this by 365 days a year, and it can be accomplished in 11.8 minutes a day. If our reading pace is slower than a professional articulator, it might take 15-20 minutes. Remember: *"A 'journey' of a thousand miles begins with a single step."*

Day-by-day and step-by-step, as we discipline ourselves and our time, and yield to the control of the Holy Spirit, the Word of Christ will begin to richly dwell within us (Col. 3:16). As we saturate our minds with God's Word and the desire to truly apply it, the Holy Spirit will produce in us: ***love, joy, peace, kindness, goodness, gentleness, patience, self-control, and faithfulness.***

Now… begin, **or continue**, your quest for excellence, even if you need the help of a caregiver.

1. Establish a daily reading plan to MAXIMIZE your life for God.

2. Research various "Through the Bible" schedules, or devise one of your own.

3. Ask a friend/family member to commit to using the same plan.

4. Discuss verses, now and then, with each other.

5. Persevere! Build on the self-control and faithfulness the Holy Spirit is producing within you.

6. Ask God to help you understand and properly apply His truth.

7. Rejoice and praise God when you finish!

8. Start again! You will never plumb the depths of God's wisdom.

Nuggets of wisdom, promises and praise:
(Sing, or simply read as prayerful poetry.)

"Wonderful Words of Life" by Philip P. Bliss

Sing them over again to me, Wonderful words of Life;
Let me more of their beauty see, Wonderful words of Life.
Words of life and beauty, Teach me faith and duty;

Refrain:
Beautiful words, wonderful words, Wonderful words of Life.
Beautiful words, wonderful words, Wonderful words of Life.

Christ, the blessed One, gives to all Wonderful words of Life;
Sinner, list' to the loving call, Wonderful words of Life.
All so freely given, wooing us to Heaven:

Refrain:
Beautiful words, wonderful words, Wonderful words of Life.
Beautiful words, wonderful words, Wonderful words of Life.

Sweetly echo the gospel call, Wonderful words of Life;
Offer pardon and peace to all, Wonderful words of Life.
Jesus, only Savior, Sanctify forever:

Refrain:
Beautiful words, wonderful words, Wonderful words of Life.
Beautiful words, wonderful words, Wonderful words of Life.

Chapter 17

Thanksgiving and Praise

Achieve a Passionate Prayer Life

pray, v.- to offer devout (earnest; fervent) petition, praise, thanks, etc. to God.
thanksgiving, n.- the act of giving thanks, especially to God, to express gratitude or appreciation.

What glory it will be to stand at the foot of the throne and feel God's love, compassion and acceptance surrounding us. What joy to see His smile smiling at *us*!

Do we want to step into His presence empty-handed? What kind of a "Hostess" gift can we take to the Creator of heaven and earth? Certainly not empty hands!

I thought about this the day I climbed the steps of the Lincoln Memorial in Washington, D.C. I stood by the foot of Lincoln and looked up at his knee. I had seen photographs of other people at the same spot, and yet nothing prepared me for the feelings that engulfed me. I was so insignificant compared to the majesty of this man-made monument. My thoughts turned to Revelation chapter four and the scene John, the writer, encounters of God's most sovereign and authoritative Throne. He saw "diamonds" refracting all the colors of the rainbow in wondrous brilliance; the hues of ruby and emerald dominated the colors surrounding the Throne. John also witnessed 24 elders (Rev. 4:4), representing the church, sitting with Christ, all clothed in pure white robes and golden crowns. These are the saints who have accepted Christ as the "Bridge" of redemption. They have been given their crowns, and are living in the place Christ had prepared for them. There is lightning and thunder (Rev. 4:5), and lamps of fire, and spirits, creatures and angels. All of these living beings are uncontrollably thanking and praising God for His glory and power.

Stepping into this scenario will make Lincoln's knee quite insignificant! I can't even fathom the idea of entering the Throne room and having the LORD Himself bend forward, smile at me, take me into His Presence, and tell me how much He loves me.

HE loves *me*!

My prayer life, and my whole life, changed dramatically once I had this scene in my head.

How could I simply "multi-task" a quick request to God? Of course He hears the softest whisper, but He has taught us to pray (Matt. 26:39 -NIV) "not my will, but Your's be done." How could I pray in a way that would please God, and not just the "hit-and-run" approach that fit my lifestyle of instant gratification?

Besides taking examples from David's beautiful, heartfelt Psalms, and other earthly prayers, I pictured myself praying in two different ways.

First, I pictured myself boldly entering heaven, grumbling, complaining and asking. I completely disregard everything that is going on, and that isn't relevant to *me* and *my* needs. I just blurt out what I want!

My second approach to the Throne I pictured much differently. I focus on God's beauty. I hear the praise and adoration that surrounds His Throne. I immediately follow the example of the 24 elders, and I can hear my own voice sing out in thanksgiving, praise, and worship (1 Thess. 5:16). I show God my heart and my love for Him, and in His presence I have no needs.

I could stay forever at the feet of Jesus, and yet I must get back to "real" life. At this point I understand the words of the Lord's prayer when He taught us that His will is to be done "on earth as it is in heaven" (Matt. 6:10). As I "see" what is happening in heaven I know what I must do. I thanked God for removing the blinders from my eyes, and I asked Him to give me a thankful heart, and teach me to replicate this scene on earth, not just in my life but also in the lives of those my life touches. May we be thankful in all things (1 Thess. 5:18).

You can imagine that once I moved from my shallow, self-centered prayers, to prayers of love and adoration, everything changed. As I read the Scriptures my eyes were suddenly filled with "Light" (Psalm 36:9). Verses that I had read many times before flooded my heart with truth and insights, wisdom and understanding. The more I read, the more I wanted to be at the foot of God's Throne in prayer. My reading and prayer became intermingled. I learned to ask Him to show me what *He* wanted me to learn. I learned to wait on Him and seek His insights, and He has never failed to give me the wisdom and understanding I need for the trouble of each day.

As I seek to obey the righteousness of God, He is faithful to provide for my every earthly need (not my greed; my need!). He is truly faithful to His promises! When He says, "Seek ye first the kingdom of God, and His righteousness, and all these thing will be added unto you" (Matthew 6:33), He means it!

"The LORD will go before you...and be your rear guard." (Isaiah 52:12b) He picks up the pieces I overlook. He holds my hand, and carries my load.

Of course, if I hold on to my load in self-sufficiency He allows me to reject His help. But He is there, watching and waiting for me to refocus, and seek His will and help. It's amazing how quickly prideful thinking can overtake us!

Sometimes when we seek an answer over and over again for a continuing problem, we learn to restate our prayers and ask the Holy Spirit to take it before the LORD. He promised in Romans 8:26-27 that the Holy Spirit prays for us in groaning much deeper than words.

Once we do this we usually see things in a different, more insightful Light, or we're given overwhelming peace and patience to wait for God's perfect timing in the matter.

I'm reminded of a message I heard from Joni Erickson Tada. She said that her prayer for 30 years, since her diving accident, was to be healed of her paralysis. During a tour of Jerusalem she related her excitement as she sat in her wheelchair at the edge of the ancient pool of healing, Bethesda (John 5:2-3). As she prayed for healing, once again, she was filled with an overwhelming understanding of God's purpose for the chair. This was her "prayer closet." She didn't have the capacity to run around doing, doing, doing. She then saw herself in a different light, God's Light. He wanted an intimate relationship with her. He gave her the gift of her own personal "prayer closet" that goes with her everywhere. It's amazing how we can think one narrow way year after year, and in a twinkling of an eye God can change our perspective.

For me, Joni is the ultimate example for facing physical trials in God's strength. Even during the difficult days of old age, most of us will never suffer the insults to our bodies that Joni has faced. We must learn, as she did, to embrace God's plan for us. In doing so we must continually pray that God will use us to even a fractional percentage of how He has used Joni. And, as Joni continues to do, we also will be filled with thankfulness and song, and our ebbing lives will encourage others to reach out and touch the very Face of God.

"In Jesus' Name, we pray." This is not a "formula" of five words that would guarantee the success of our requests. "Jesus' Name" means the *will* He has for us is to glorify that Name, through the days of plenty, and the days of evil. Everything else is vanity!

But old age is hard! What if we forget? What if the pain is unbearably distracting? Solomon seems to think it could be. Who are we to argue with God's Word, and try to minimize the effects of aging on the body and mind?

Solomon also tells us there is a time for everything, and God has made everything beautiful in its time (Eccl. 3:1-11), and in 1 Corinthians 10:13 God tells us that nothing will come to us that is not common to "men." He promises He will provide a way of escape, not from the challenges, but from negative, non-productive reactions to them.

This is where we can really start preparing and practicing for the future. Mark 6:7 states the prudent practice of "going out" two-by-two, which provides mutual help and encouragement. Now is the time to develop a "two-by-two" relationship with someone we love who loves us and knows us deeply. Then we will be ready to practice this principle during all our "difficult days."

The person we choose could be anyone we trust to keep our deepest thoughts and concerns completely private. It's also someone we talk with on a daily or weekly basis; someone who has our, and God's, best interest at heart. We can make a lifetime pact with this person to uphold each other in daily prayer, and always focus on how we each can best glorify God's Name (Eccl. 4:12).

We can pray that we will each be a blessing, especially in kind and gentle speech (James 3:8-12; Col. 4:6; Eph. 4:31-32).

"The effectual fervent prayer of a righteous 'man' avails much" (James 5:16).

One of our most fervent prayers for each other should be that as we finish the "race" we will:

- have a Godly, not evil, influence on our-worlds.
- be peaceable.
- be gentle.
- be willing to yield.

And we should pray for God's wisdom that is:

- pure.
- full of mercy and good "fruit."
- impartial and, above all, *not* hypocritical (James 3:17).

If we are energetic, fervent and passionate as we seek God's help for each other, we are assured that He hears us and loves to answer (Psalm 34:15).

Once we've established one or two passionate prayer partners, we can enlarge our circle of prayer a little more. As we interact with our world we can humbly ask that they specifically pray that we will always magnify God's Name until the day He takes us "home." Unfortunately, many people get into a very negative cycle at this point, and blame their failures and inadequacies on the aging process. I pray that we will learn to accept the process, and ask others to pray that as we outwardly waste away, we will be renewed inwardly, day by day (2 Cor. 4:16).

After we find our own "voice" of prayer, and ask a couple of trusted friends (or relatives) to pray for our deepest needs, and seek prayer from the rest of our family and friends, we can take it one step further. Every "silver" saint can start praying for our whole army of "silver" saints as we march (limp?) through the lives of our worlds, and on to the Goal. Christ did not tell us to pray exclusively for ourselves. He taught (Matt. 6:11-13) us to pray, "give *us* this day *our* daily bread… Lead *us* not into temptation, but deliver *us* from *evil*." (There's that evil wolf, again!)

What if we all took that to heart? First, we would have to put aside our own narrow self-concerns, and realize that thousands (millions?) of "silver" saints are experiencing almost a carbon copy of what we are going through. If we all make a pact, right now, to pray for one another, just think of the positive, glorifying heritage our generation could pass down to the generations to come. Think of the daily praise that would be going to the foot of the Throne, not just from our lips, but also from the lips of our children, our family and friends, and our caretakers.

As our worlds experience God's love and goodness through us, they will either thank God for us, or thank us. If they thank us, we in turn can thank God for making it possible to magnify His character. Our thankfulness is the "hostess" gift we can give to our Heavenly Father as we—

"Come before His presence with singing...
enter into His gates with ***thanksgiving****,*
and into His courts with ***praise****,*
...His truth endures to all generations." (Psalm 100)

Our greatest desire should be to become the golden link between our precious LORD, and the next generation. And then our greatest joy will be watching our families, our-worlds, praise and adore Him.

O Father,

As I come before You today, my heart is overflowing with joy! You have filled me with gladness! These simple words cannot express my thankfulness for being one of Your "sheep," so well taken care of in Your "pasture." (Psalm 100:3) *Protected from the wolf! Fill me LORD, and let praise for You be continually in my mouth. As my-world hears of it let them in turn, be glad. Bind us in unity as we magnify, and exalt Your Name together.* (Psalm 34:1-3)

Help us to remember to pray for one another. Lead me to someone who will commit to praying for me, daily, as I pray for him/her while we pass through the "fire" of old age. Remind me to hold all Your "silver" saints close to my heart as we "march" through the last days of our lives reflecting You. Prepare us, and refine us. Let us collectively make an overwhelming show of Your love, truth, kindness and goodness, gentleness, mercy and good "fruit."

May we all one day stand before Your mighty Throne, and hear You say, 'Well done, you allowed Me to shine through the hardest time of your earthly stay" (Daniel 12:3).

Claim Your Gold

Application Guide

Engrave your heart:
(Memorize, or simply re-read during the day.)

"Continue earnestly in ***prayer****, being vigilant in it with thanksgiving."*
-Colossians 4:2

"Your will be done on earth as it is in heaven." -Matthew 6:10

"Rejoice ALWAYS, ***pray*** *without ceasing, in everything give thanks; for this is the will of God in Christ Jesus for you."*
-1 Thessalonians 5:16-18

"The effective, fervent ***prayer*** *of a righteous "man" avails much."*
-James 5:16

Refine the gold:

I would venture to say that 99.9% of us have asked God, at one time or another, for something during a "9-1-1" crisis. Or maybe we've asked Him for direction, or for some material blessing that we tried to convince Him would make us love Him more.

Through studies and surveys about the prayer habits of professing Christians it has been revealed that the average person prays less than five minutes a day. Even among pastors and their wives the average was seven minutes. Of course, to have an "average" there are many who pray much more than five minutes balancing those who pray much less.

When I was a new Christian I was in the Five-Minutes-or-Less Club. Why should I spend time praying when I knew God already knew what I needed? What a waste of time!

The year I started reading through the Bible the Scriptures concerning "prayer" jumped off the page at me. There were so many of them! Many of which commanded us to pray. My confusion grew. Why did God need me to ask Him for things He already had planned? I was committed to reading and obeying God's Word, and since it told me to pray I decided to do it with all my heart.

As I obediently set out to follow God's Word and Christ's example in the area of prayer, I decided to record the results of my obedience. I started using a personal prayer journal to record my prayers, and the results of my prayers.

However, I was in the Five-Minute Club! What did I have to say that anyone would care about? How do you start writing to God? Writing was so much harder than just quickly rattling off a few words. Nevertheless, I was determined to grow in obedience and so I began. My words were choppy and few, but I took the first step in what has proven to be an incredible journey to the Heart of God.

My dreaded five minutes have turned into unlimited, constant access to the Throne of my LORD, my Savior, my Father, my Friend. Over the years my shaky journaling has blossomed into incredible love letters of praise, honor and thanksgiving to the Lover of my soul. What if I had stubbornly continued in my own way of thinking and refused to obey in faith? I would have missed out on this incredible relationship.

Prayer is ***not*** simply an ask, seek, and knock tool, even though it is available to us for that purpose as Luke 11:9 tells us. Prayer is our way of honoring God with our praise and thankfulness. It is a direct and instant conduit for our language of love.

Imagine for a moment that you have two grown children that you love with all your heart. Your greatest desire would be to have that love returned. The first child calls you with a quick request when a need arises. The second child, on the other hand, pours out his/her love upon you in daily phone calls that fill your heart with joy. Child number two has fulfilled you greatest hope of parenthood. Which "child" would fulfill God's greatest desires for beloved communication?

God created us for companionship and love. Our purpose on earth from the very beginning has always been, *"You shall **love** the LORD your God with all your heart, with all your soul, and with all your mind..."* (Matt. 22:37) All the people, angels, creatures surrounding the throne in heaven are doing that at this very moment, and every moment.

Do heavenly beings hear our prayers? Do they praise God when they hear of our love and praise for God? Is our honor to our Father multiplied on their lips? On the other hand, how does heaven deal with our quick, demanding, manipulative tones? Awesome thoughts to research and contemplate as we try to replicate God's will on earth as The Lord's Prayer (Matt. 6:9-13) teaches us to do.

Prayer that is effective, fervent, vigilant, earnest and continuous takes practice and planning.

1. Examine your prayer life in God's truth.

2. Purpose in your heart to MAXIMIZE this cornerstone of a righteous "man."
3. Obtain a good Study Bible, Concordance and/or Bible Software.

4. Research all the verses concerning "Prayer." (There are many!)

5. Set aside an exact time each day that you will meet with your LORD. Pencil it in on your calendar if you must!

6. Keep your appointment, just as you would any other appointment. If you must cancel, *immediately* reschedule another time.

7. Take the challenge! Start a Prayer Journal even if it only consists of one or two sentences a day.
8. Collect pictures of people in your-world, and start a prayer file.
   - Glue pictures to file cards, or notebook pages.
   - On each card, or page record his/her name, relationship, email address, address, birthday, and other *information you might need if your memory starts to fade a bit.*
   - Schedule a time (once a week; every day) to pray for his/her specific needs, as you hold them (his/her picture) in your hand and in your heart.
   - Send notes (email is also good) of encouragement and love.
   - Send birthday cards, and stay connected.
   - When people ask you what you want for your birthday, Christmas or other holidays offer practical suggestions, such as:
     - » A new calendar with all family birthdays boldly marked.
     - » Note cards and assorted greeting cards.
     - » Pre-made address labels of family members.
     - » Stamps.
     - » Two new photographs; one to display, and one for your file, or notebook.
     - » A new journal.

9. Start building prayer support.
   - Ask a close friend or relative, or two, to be your prayer partner now and through out the coming years. Share your deepest concerns, and commit to pray for one another.
   - Ask your family and friends to pray for your faithfulness in glorifying God's Holy Name all the days of your life. In return, keep each family member before the Throne of God.
   - Pray earnestly for every "silver" saint who is facing this path, common to "man," to magnify God's character daily.

10. Thank God ***always***… for ***everything***, and ***everyone***!

Nuggets of wisdom, promises and praise:
(Sing, or simply read as prayerful poetry.)

"May Jesus Christ Be Praised" by Katholisches Gesangbuch *(translated by Edward Caswall)*

When morning gilds the skies, My heart awaking cries,
May Jesus Christ be praised!
Alike at work or prayer To Jesus I repair,
May Jesus Christ be praised!

The night becomes as day, when from the heart we say,
May Jesus Christ be praised!
The pow'rs of darkness fear when this sweet chant they hear,
May Jesus Christ be praised!

Ye nations of mankind, in this your concord find,
May Jesus Christ be praised!
Let all the earth around Ring joyously with sound,
May Jesus Christ be praised!

Be this, while life is mine, My canticle divine,
May Jesus Christ be praised!
Be this th'eternal song thro' all the ages long,
May Jesus Christ be praised!

Chapter 18

Communicate Masterfully

Utilize the Power of God's Loving Spirit

alchemist, n.- a person versed in the practice of converting ordinary materials into gold.

As I lean closer to the mirror I try to deny the truth of my reflection, but the Holy Spirit brings a verse to my mind... *"And the LORD said to him (Joshua), 'Thou art* **old** *and stricken in years'"* (Joshua 13:1 -KJV).

Ouch! Talk about seeking the truth, and the truth will set me free! God Himself confirms it; I am old! But the verse that flooded through my mind didn't stop there. The remaining part of the passage gave me hope for the future. *"...there remains very much land yet to be possessed."*

God faithfully empowered Joshua to fulfill His plan of conquering the Promised Land. Joshua could have received God's proclamation that he was *old* with bitterness. He could have decided to just sit down in the gloom of his self-made "train station," and wait for the "train" of the grim reaper.

"Sitting at the station" is a quote I've heard come from the lips of professing Christian men and women, as they go through this time. They are just waiting... waiting for the "grim reaper."

Dr. C. W. Smith was refined gold! As a professor at a Christian college, he was not among those who just waited at the "station." Dr. Smith was a mighty man of God. During his bout with a very deadly form of cancer, he made it a high priority to multiply the "time and space" he had been given. He pushed past his chemo-induced fatigue, and actively and purposefully reached out in love, kindness, and great humility to his world. As he went through his last days with his family and friends he gathered a large crowd of seekers. His reflected image of God's peace and grace was so overwhelming, and motivating, people were drawn to his "saltiness." Surrounded by multitudes (many who, like Job's wife, could *not* see God in the process (Job 2:9)), he could have uttered negative, discouraging words that would have stolen glory from God. But, in his weakness and lessened physical ability, all of the promises proclaimed in the Scriptures were highly magnified in his life.

God tells us in 2 Corinthians 12:9, "My strength is made perfect in weakness." We seem to think it is only while we are young and strong that God can use us. Over and over again He tells us He doesn't depend on the strength of horses, "men," chariots, or any earthly power (Psalm 147:10-11, Psalm 33:16-17, Zech. 4:6). His greatest moments are when people come to the end of themselves and their strength and look to Him (Psalm 33:16-22, Psalm 34).

Dr. Smith adamantly warned Christians not to "cop out" by telling everyone they are "waiting on the LORD." That sounds very spiritual, but grumbling and complaining as we just wait to die has never been part of God's plan for anyone.

A man who tried to "sit it out" was Jonah. God had plans for him, but in his rebellion, and disobedience against God's plan for his life, he hopped on a ship and was headed 180-degrees from God's will (Jonah 1:3). He even tried to hide in the "train station" at the bottom of his escape vessel (Jonah 1:5).

One thing in his favor was that he proclaimed his love for "the LORD, the God of heaven, who made the sea and the land" (Jonah 1:9). Jonah knew he was being disobedient, and as the fury of the storm tossed the ship around, his guilty feelings increased.

We can just imagine what Jonah might of thought; *I know what I will do! I'll show these fearful sailors a very spiritual, self-sacrificing act. I'll 'kill two birds with one stone.' When they throw me overboard to save the ship from God's wrath, they'll see just how brave I am, and... when I'm drowned, I won't have to go to Nineveh and do God's work.*

Sometimes readers think of the dark, wet belly of the great fish as a grim punishment, but in God's goodness He sent the fish for Jonah's protection. In the darkness of his new "God-given prayer-closet" Jonah reprioritized his thinking as he called out to God (Jonah 2:1-10).

Jonah was given a second chance to obey. The pagan sailors, and the pagan city of Nineveh (about 230 miles north of present-day Baghdad) miraculously responded to the message God had commissioned reluctant Jonah to deliver. In Jonah's weakness God's strength prevailed.

Jonah's story does not end there. He was angry with God for sending salvation to the Gentiles. He was extremely displeased with God's gracious compassion and mercy for these evil "outsiders" (4:1-2).

He actually asked the LORD, *"please take my life from me, for it is better for me to die than to live"* (4:3).

Jonah was self-consumed! All he wanted was a shady place to sit and watch what would happen to the city. Jonah turned his faith into "people watching," and grumbling against God. But Christianity is not a spectator sport. We are *in* the race! We have a job to do, and we are to "run" with endurance, keeping our eyes on Christ. With Christ as our example we see that it was not until He endured the cross and finished the course set before Him that He sat down (Heb. 12:1-2). It's not finished until God says it's finished!

Jonah could have sought God's will for the next step, but instead, he admonished God for His mercy to thousands and thousands of people. *"Where's Your mercy for me?"* Jonah whined, *"I'm hot!"*... *"It is better for me to die than to live."* Three times Jonah asked to die, but God had a plan for his life. Instead of receiving God's blessing for his obedience, Jonah was lectured by God for his self-centeredness, and lack of love (4:10).

God will "take care of business" and fulfill His will. But, *we* have a choice! We can be blessed by Him for our obedience, and return that blessing to Him in the form of thankful adoration, or we can choose to be "lectured" by Him, and returned to our "path" to live out the days He has planned for us.

As we spend our last days praising, and glorifying God, He will pour out blessings on our weakness.

We can claim the promises of Psalm 92:12-14,

"The righteous ***shall flourish*** *like a palm tree,*
He shall grow like a cedar in Lebanon.
Those who are planted in the house of the LORD
shall flourish *in the courts of our God.*
They shall ***bear fruit*** *in* ***old age****;*
they shall be fresh and flourishing,
to declare that the LORD is upright..."

If we stay "planted" in the courtyard of the LORD, and the thriving conditions of a close relationship with Him, we will produce abundant fruit. Our-world will see, and feel the love, kindness, gentleness, peace and joy that God has promised all who believe and submit.

When I read this verse I picture a healthy, tall, green date palm reaching to the sun. Clusters of golden fruit are continually being produced and gobbled up by a hungry world. That's what I want to "look" like in my old age. I want to saturate my world with the golden fruit of the Holy Spirit working in my life.

*"****Whatever*** *you do, do all to the glory of God"* (1 Cor. 10:31).

"Whatever I do" will be determined, pretty much, by the parts of my body that remain useable during those last days. I know that whatever I am left with will be my "talent," assigned to me, and if I ask, God will enable me to focus on making the most of what He allows me to use.

> *"My flesh and my heart may **fail** me,*
> ***but God** is the strength of my heart and*
> *my portion forever"* (Psalm 73:26).

It is very possible that our only working body member will be our tongues. Maybe that is why there are so many Scriptures that instruct us on the use of our mouths, lips and tongue (Psalm 66:17-18; 141:3; Prov. 30:32; 31:26; I Peter 3:10; James 3:3-12). The tongue is compared to a tiny rudder of a ship. It steers the course of not only the ship, but all the people on board (James 3:4-5).

Whatever our age, the tongue reflects the inside of our "cup," our heart (Luke 6:45). Are the words of our mouths showy, little wildflowers, here one moment, gone the next, making a seasonal display as we share our "spiritual sound-bites." Or, do our words take root in living water (John 7:37-38), and tap the very heart of God?

*"Either make a tree good and its **fruit** will be good, or else make the tree bad and its **fruit** bad; for every tree is known by its **fruit**... For out of the abundance of the heart the mouth speaks... For by your **words** you will be justified, and by your **words*** (even a slip-of-the-tongue) *you will be condemned"* (Matt. 12:33-37).

It's obvious we have our work cut out for us! Undoubtedly, we all have had to face the results of a slip-of-the-tongue, but, if we confess our unloving words, or even the tone or attitude of our words, the LORD is faithful to forgive us. He is also faithful in leading us to change, if we are willing to continually examine our ways, and evaluate them against the standards of Scripture.

When I think about examining myself on a continuous basis, I think of Christ's yearly trips to the temple for Passover. Mary and Joseph were righteous, obedient Jews. They religiously followed God's plan for worship as they traveled to Jerusalem, year after year, for special holy days. Jesus must have walked through the courts of the temple every year and witnessed the abuse and the gouging of the poor as the moneychangers charged high fees to make possible the purchase of an appropriate sacrifice for the ceremony. Did Jesus ever discuss this with His parents, or ever bring it up as He taught in the synagogue at the age of 12? We may never know, but we can be sure this practice did not go unnoticed. Even though the Bible says nothing about His next 18 years, it seems safe to assume that Jesus continued to accompany His parents to His Father's temple.

At age 30 He launched His earthly ministry, and reminded the people of all they had been taught through the prophets of the Old Testament. He summarized the principles contained in the Law and the Prophets with one short statement, the Golden Rule—"*Therefore, whatever you want men to do to you, do also to them, for this is the Law and the Prophets*" (Matt. 7:12). He expanded the concept of loving others by reminding them that they were to care for the poor and needy.

The Pharisees and Scribes were insulted! They knew the Scriptures! And yet, year after year, they never examined their practice of "ripping off" the poor. They knew the Word, but they didn't *do* the Word!

One of Christ's first actions, recorded in John 2:14-16, was to drive the moneychangers from the outer courts of the temple. How long had He wanted to do this? How long would the results of His action last? Not long! Just three short years later, during His last week on earth, He again does the job the Pharisees and Scribes should have been doing. They should have examined their own practices to see if they were truly following the Scriptures. Christ was probably more angry this second time He cleansed His temple, for He had made it crystal clear the first time. Their practices dishonored God's Word! If they wouldn't examine themselves and obey, He would do it for them.

Do we need the Holy Spirit to come to our hearts (His temple) and do this work for us? He will! As we mature, we seek our own flaws. We learn to ask God to show us where we are falling short of His will. His goal is to mold us into His image. That includes every part of His image, even His "tongue," and His gentle, loving, kind manner.

The fruit of the tongue can undermine, and tear down our own carefully built home, or it can edify and build-up for the generations to come (Proverbs 14:1; 16:21-24; 25:11; Eph. 4:29-32).

In education, studies of the brain have opened-up some enormous learning concepts. We now know that in order to make a skill become an automatic response, it must be taught, or revisited, through varying methods, an average of 24 times. On the other hand, when we hear or see something incorrectly, only *one* time, it takes at least seven correct teachings to simply "erase" the negative input. We have to do that before we can start building on the positive.

These new insights have far reaching implications, and they give us clear direction for lesson planning.

As we contemplated these statistics we can apply them to the "fruit" of the tongue, and the building up, or tearing down of our own home (Prov. 14:1-3).

Twenty-four times of speaking positive, edifying, loving, kind words builds a relationship of trust. Just one slip-of-the-tongue, or negative, grumbling, complaining sentence, can, of course, be forgiven, but it will take many "positives" before trust is re-established.

What if we are brave enough to examine ourselves on a daily basis, and find that we are grumblers and negative, undermining complainers? What if we count the sentences we utter in just one day, and discover an attitude and tone of discontentment? Multiply each negative statement times seven to calculate how many times we will have to express contentment and joy before our world will trust our positive words.

For some of us the number will be staggering and seem impossible to correct. But even in the latest stages of life God can make new creations, and even renew the minds of those we have infected. That is the beauty of God's power in our weakness. If we are willing, "… with God, all things are possible" (Matt. 19:26).

God's equation for our future is simple if we allow Him to be our Alchemist.

G O D + O L D = G O L D

We have the secret for becoming a new creation (2 Cor. 5:17) and finding, and refining the gold for the "Golden Years." Galatians 2:20

says: *"I have been crucified with Christ: it is no longer I who live, but* ***Christ lives in me****...."*

Jesus can change us just as He changed the water into wine during a wedding in Cana of Galilee (John 2:3-10). The most encouraging part of that story, for us, is that the wedding guests were amazed that the ***best,*** most perfect wine was saved until last.

If each of us puts our life into His Hands, our last days can be our ***best*** days, and our world can send us off in joy, across the "Bridge" of Christ, and into the waiting arms of the Creator of the universe, and the Lover of our soul. And as our physical world shrinks to the size of a casket-shaped box, our love will live on! All the hearts whose lives we've touched will be as Noah's family—eager and ready to follow us to God's magnificent rainbow.

"When He has tested me, I shall come forth as gold."
-Job 23:10

O Father,

Thank You for this exciting, new outlook on receiving a frail, weakened body, and equally frail mind. I pray that Your beauty will be overwhelmingly magnified in my frailties and weakness. Renew my mind on a daily basis, and give me the self-control it will take to stay focused through the bad times.

Take my fear of failure, and fill me with Your confidence and perseverance.

I love You, LORD! And my greatest desire is to know that my-world will love You, too.

Touch my tongue that I might speak only edifying words of love, wisdom and truth. "You taught me from my youth; and to this day I declare Your wondrous works. Now, also, when I am old... do not forsake me, until I declare Your strength to this generation, Your power to everyone who is to come" (Psalm 71:17-18).

May I, one day, stand before Your glorious Throne, and hear You say, "Well done... You magnified and glorified My Name (Psalm 34:3). *You sought My will, and My perfecting power, you stayed the course, and YOU became the GOLD in your 'Golden Years!'"* (Psalm 1:1-3)

Claim Your Gold

Application Guide

Engrave your heart:
(Memorize, or simply re-read during the day.)

"Let nothing be done through selfish ambition or conceit,
but in lowliness of mind let each esteem ***others*** *better than "himself."*
Let each of you look out not only for "his" own interest,
but also for the interests of ***others****."*
-Philippians 2:3-4

"Therefore, whatever you want "men" to do to you,
do *also to them,*
for this is the Law and the Prophets."
-Matthew 7:12

"Either make a tree good and its ***fruit*** *will be good,*
or else make the tree bad and its fruit bad;
for every tree is known by its fruit...
For out of the abundance of the heart the ***mouth*** *speaks...*
For by your words you will be justified,
and by your words you will be condemned." -Matthew 12:33-37

Refine the gold:

Through all my years of professional development and leadership training for teachers and principals, we were constantly being bombarded with little games that were designed to help us connect with each other. God's principle of relating well with ***others*** penetrates all human activity. From large corporations to tiny family units, most people see the value in perfecting this skill.

Many of the exercises that were planned to develop "one another" skills were based on verbal communication and body language. The purpose, of course, was to raise productivity in the work place. The theory being that as colleagues learn to listen to each other, focus on ***"heart"*** meaning and not on just the words, and speak kindly and to the point, and ***not*** to their own agendas, true communication will take place, and consequently production will increase in a peaceful and respectful environment.

One of the most dramatic methods for instilling these communication concepts was an exercise called *The Fish Bowl.*

We watched as half of the first group of "players" sat in a discussion circle; the other half sat behind a partner, as observers. The observers, with clipboards in hand, documented the communication skills of their partners.

A controversial subject was introduced in the discussion circle. Everyone was on his or her most polite conversational behavior (everyone had been briefed on the skills, and the carefully designed checklist being used). You would think that with all this preparation, and this "crowd of witnesses," the communication skills would have been exemplary. You would be wrong!

Once a nerve was hit, the gloves came off (for a few)! **Their** individual viewpoints soon became more important than the purpose of the "test." As the pressure increased, false niceness quickly disappeared. All kindness, patience, and gentle tones flew out the window! The observers had trouble keeping up with recording all of the negative input.

When it was finally our turn to "play," we, the teachers, were each sitting with the principal from our own school. We listened carefully as the trainers gave us the extensive checklist of negative and positive communication skills. We were then told that we would be "grading" our own **boss** as the principals discussed the issue of whether or not schools should be integrated using the busing of students to achieve racial balance.

This was already a hot topic in the district, but the purpose of the exercise was NOT to solve the problem, but to share ideas and insights in an **edifying, bridge-building** approach.

As the principals began, the rhetoric, sarcasm and eye rolling soon found their way into the circle, and all the teachers were struggling to walk in truth; should we tell it like it happened, or fudge on the facts for the sake of job security? The trainers called a time-out and encouraged us to be truthful, and then, with great wisdom, they had us all shift seats, and evaluate someone other than our own boss.

After 15 minutes of hot debate, time was called and we, the observers, debriefed with our partners, and then the last 15 minutes began. Was there improvement? In a few cases there was! But, most quickly fell back into well-worn paths of **negative, devaluating** "communication."

This eye opening "test" started my "what-ifing." Would we dare to replicate this in our church groups and families? Would believers display the fruit of the Spirit that they have proclaimed, or would they be the first to fall into the temptation of flaunting their own personal "wisdom?" In an effort to be right, would they squelch the spirit of their "listeners?"

If we truly desire to fulfill God's one another purpose for our lives, we must earnestly seek to make ***meaningful*** connections.

Anyone can spout off with seemingly right-on statements, but it takes a "mouth" completely submitted to Christ's example and the power of the Holy Spirit to perfectly connect, heart-to-heart with another human being.

1. Plan a "fish bowl" experience of your own by enlisting the help of a trusted family member, or your prayer partner, and agree to lovingly listen to each other's corrective suggestions.

2. In every conversation pay attention, with your heart, and watch for body language. Is your "listener" just being polite? Tune-in! Focus on ***connecting*** with the other person and not just talking ***at*** them. ***Listen*** twice as much as you speak ("two ears; one mouth").

3. Apply all the fruit of the Spirit (***love, joy, peace, patience, kindness, goodness, faithfulness, gentleness and self-control***), through the power of the Holy Spirit, in every conversation.

4. Ask the Holy Spirit to be your Observer in all your conversations, and to alert you to your negative and/or unloving communication throughout the day. (He IS observing whether we ask, or not, but we are told to ***ask***.)

5. ***Submit*** to His debriefings. If you truly seek to improve in this area of your walk, the LORD will speak to your heart. And once He does, ***confess*** your unloving attitude and/or words, and **ask for forgiveness** from God and from the one you've offended.

6. Research every Scripture that deals with ***fools***, and the ***folly*** of their mouths, and their lives. There are many in Proverbs. (Proverbs 12:15; 15:2; 17:4, 9; 26:24-26, 28; etc.)

7. Contrast that by researching all the passages that draw a picture for us of each Spirit-filled "fruit" as related to the tongue.

– Love: I Corinthians 13:1-7…
– Joy: Proverbs 15:23…
– Peace: James 3:17-18…
– Kindness: I Corinthians 13:4…
– Gentleness: II Timothy 2:24
– Goodness: I Thessalonians 5:15, 21…

– Patience: I Thessalonians 5:14…
– Faithfulness: Psalm 119:112…
– Self-control: II Peter 1:5-7…

8. Ask God to help you to truly connect with the ***next*** person on your path ***today*** (even if you're too busy for a long conversation).

9. Be interested in others; tell ***your*** "stories" ***only*** when you can reflect God's goodness for ***their*** current situation.

10. Thank God for deep, meaningful, life-changing relationships.

Nuggets of promises and praise:
(Sing, or simply read as prayerful poetry.)

"Standing on the Promises" by R. Kelso Carter

Standing on the promises of Christ my King,
Thro' eternal ages let His praises ring;
Glory in the highest, I will shout and sing,
Standing on the promises of God.
Refrain:
Standing, standing,
I'm standing on the promises of God my Savior;
Standing, standing,
I'm standing on the promises of God.

Standing on the promises that cannot fail,
When the howling storms of doubt and fear assail,
By the living Word of God I shall prevail,
Standing on the promises of God.
Refrain

Standing on the promises of Christ the LORD,
Bound to Him eternally by love's strong cord,
Overcoming daily with the Spirit's sword,
Standing on the promises of God.
Refrain

Standing on the promises I cannot fall,
List'ning every moment to the Spirits call,
Resting in my Savior as my all in all,
Standing on the promises of God.
Refrain

Epilogue

Hope

hope, n.- a person or thing in which expectations are centered.

I cannot close and leave the wolf from Chapter Two in charge! Little Red Riding Hood and her precious Grandmother were last seen being swallowed by that frightful wolf. But hope springs eternal, for the faithful *Huntsman* is constantly on guard.

As Jonah was sheltered in the dark belly of the great fish, so Lil' Red and Grandma were gluttonously swallowed whole. By using His mighty *Sword*, the *Huntsman* quickly killed the wolf and carefully cut open his distended stomach. Little Red nimbly jumped out and gave a thankful cry. Next, grandmother slowly emerged, frightened and exhausted, but overwhelmed with gratitude.

Praising the skill and compassion of the *Huntsman* they thanked Him with truly grateful hearts, knowing it was through His power and mercy that they had been saved. And in the process of getting to know the *Huntsman*, Grandma was amazingly transformed, and overflowed with kind and gentle words of love.

As they sat together eating fresh bread, sweet butter, cookies and blackberry tea, their blissful, edifying and uplifting conversation filled the tiny cottage with joy.

Engrave your heart:
(and ***Remember***!)

*"**The LORD is my Shepherd**; I shall not want.*
He makes me lie down in green pastures;
He leads me beside the still waters. He restores my soul;
He leads me in the paths of righteousness for His Name's sake.
Yea, though I walk through the valley of the shadow of death,
***I will fear no evil** for You are with me;*
Your rod and Your staff, they comfort me.
You prepare a table before me in the presence of my enemies;
You anoint my head with oil my cup runs over.
Surely goodness and mercy will follow me ALL the days of my life;
*And **I will dwell in the house of the LORD forever**."* -Psalm 23

"Love the LORD, all His saints! The LORD preserves the faithful...
***Be strong and take heart**, All you who hope in the LORD."*
-Psalm 31:23-24 (NIV)

*"Some trust in chariots and some in horses, but **we trust in the Name of the LORD our God**... We rise up and stand firm."*
-Psalm 20:7-8 (NIV)

"My grace is sufficient for you,
*for **My strength is made PERFECT in weakness...***
That is why, for Christ's sake, I delight in weaknesses... in difficulties.
For when I am weak, then I am strong." -2 Corinthians 12:9-10

Nuggets of promises and praise:
(Sing, or simply read as prayerful poetry.)

"God Will Take Care of You" by Civilla D. Martin

Be not dismayed whatever betide, God will take care of you;
Beneath His wings of love abide, God will take care of you.
Refrain:
God will take care of you, Through every day, o'er all the way;
He will take care of you, God will take care of you.

Through days of toil when heart doth fail, God will take care of you;
When dangers fierce your path assails, God will take care of you.
Refrain:
God will take care of you, Through every day, o'er all the way;
He will take care of you, God will take care of you.

All you may need He will provide, God will take care of you;
Nothing you need will be denied, God will take care of you.
Refrain:
God will take care of you, Through every day, o'er all the way;
He will take care of you, God will take care of you.

No matter what may be the test, God will take care of you;
Lean, weary one, upon His breast, God will take care of you.
Refrain:
God will take care of you, Through every day, o'er all the way;
He will take care of you, God *will* take care of you.

"Jesus Loves Me" by Anna B. Wagner, altered

Jesus loves me! This I know, For the Bible tells me so;
Little ones to Him belong, They are weak but He is strong.
Refrain:
Yes, Jesus loves me! Yes Jesus loves me!
Yes Jesus loves me! The Bible tells me so.

Jesus loves me! He who died Heaven's gates to open wide;
He will wash away my sin, Let His little child come in.
Refrain:
Yes, Jesus loves me! Yes Jesus loves me!
Yes Jesus loves me! The Bible tells me so.

Jesus loves me! He will stay Close beside me all the way;
He's prepared a home for me, And some day His face I'll see.
Refrain:
Yes, Jesus loves me! Yes Jesus loves me!
Yes Jesus loves me! The Bible tells me so.

Bibliography

Adams, J. (1973), *The Christian Counselor's Manual*
Michigan: Zondervan Publishing House

Connolly, P. (1999), *Living in the Time of Jesus of Nazareth*
Israel: Steimatzky LTD

George, E. (1994), *Loving God with All Your Mind*
Oregon: Harvest House Publishers

Hyman, T (1983), *Little Red Riding Hood* (Brothers Grimm)
New York: Holiday House

Karssen, G. (1975), *Her Name is Woman-Book One*
Colorado: NavPress Publishing Group

Karssen, G. (1975), *Her Name is Woman-Book Two*
Colorado: NavPress Publishing Group

Keller, P. (1970), *A Shepherd Looks at Psalm 23*
Michigan: Zondervan Publishing House

MacArthur, J. (1997), *The MacArthur Study Bible-NKJV*
Tennessee: Word Bibles

MacArthur, J. (2002), *Twelve Ordinary Men*
Tennessee: W Publishing Group

MacArthur, J. (2001), *Truth For Today*
Tennessee: J. Countryman

Marzano, R., & Pickering, D., & Pollock J. (2001), *Classroom Instruction That Works.* Virginia: Association for Supervision and Curriculum Development

Morris, H. (2002), *Days of Praise*
California: Institute For Creation Research

Morris, H. M. (1976), *The Genesis Record*
Michigan: Baker Book House

Piper, J. (2003), *Don't Waste Your Life*
Illinois: Crossway Books

Spenger, M. (1999), *Learning and Memory- The Brain in Action*
Virginia: Association for Supervision and Curriculum Development

Swindoll, C. (1985), *Living on the Ragged Edge*
Dallas: Word Publishing

Tyndale (1986), *The One-Year Bible, New International Version*
Illinois: Tyndale House Publishers, Inc.

Tyndale (2000), Touch Points BIBLE PROMISES
Illinois: Tyndale House Publishers, Inc.

Whitney, D. S. (2002), Spiritual Disciplines for the Christian Life Colorado: NavPress Publishing Group

28885486R00124

Made in the USA
Columbia, SC
26 October 2018